Collins

GCSE Home Economics

Child
Development
for OCR

Mark Walsh and Janet Stearns

Published by Collins Education
An imprint of HarperCollins Publishers
77-85 Fulham Palace Road
Hammersmith
London
W6 8JB

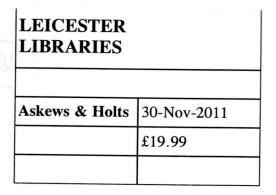

Browse the complete Collins Education catalogue at
www.collinseducation.com

ISBN 978 0 00 734271 6

Janet Stearns and Mark Walsh assert the moral right to be identified as the authors of this work.

British Library Cataloguing in Publication Data.
A Catalogue record for this publication is available from the British Library.

Commissioned by Emma Woolf
Project managed and edited by Jo Kemp
Design and typesetting by Thomson Digital
Text design by Nigel Jordan
Cover design by Angela English
Artwork by Jerry Fowler and Stella Macdonald
Index by Christine Boylan
Picture research by Geoff Holdsworth/Pictureresearch.co.uk
Printed and bound by L.E.G.O. S.p.A. Italy

Contents

Photographic acknowledgements

iStockphoto (1/H-Gall); iStockphoto (2/Ron Hope); iStockphoto (3/Sean Locke); iStockphoto (8/Hope Milam); Rex Features (9/Burger/Phanie); iStockphoto (11/Shelly Perry); Rex Features (13/Humberto Carreno); iStockphoto (15tl/NuStock); iStockphoto (15tc/ziggymaj); iStockphoto (15tr/Josh Hodge); iStockphoto (15bl/diego cervo); iStockphoto (15br/Kelvin Jay Wakefield); iStockphoto (16/Cat London); iStockphoto (18/Tomaz Levstek); Rex Features (19/Garo/Phanie); Alamy (20/imagebroker); iStockphoto (23/Aldo Murillo); iStockphoto (24/Max Delson Martins Santos); iStockphoto (25t/Dana Spiropoulou); Alamy (25b/Bildagentur-online); iStockphoto (26/Elena Korenbaum); Alamy (29/PHOTOTAKE Inc.); Alamy (30/Steve Allen); iStockphoto (31b/Carlos Gawronski); iStockphoto (31tl/Susan Trigg); iStockphoto (31tr/Elena Schweitzer); Alamy (32/Janine Wiedel Photolibrary); iStockphoto (33/Isabelle Limbach); Alamy (34t/Sally and Richard Greenhill); iStockphoto (34b/tomczykbartek); Alamy (37/Angela Hampton Picture Library); Rex Features (39t/Burger/Phanie); Alamy (39b/Mira); iStockphoto (40/Jill Lang); iStockphoto (41/Amanda Rohde); iStockphoto (42t/Kriss Russell); iStockphoto (42b/Chris Bernard); iStockphoto (43t/Dean Mitchell); Alamy (43b/Sally and Richard Greenhill); iStockphoto (44/Catharina van den Dikkenberg); iStockphoto (45/Rosemarie Gearhart); iStockphoto (46/Todd Bates); iStockphoto (47/Don Bayley); iStockphoto (48t/Beyza Sultan Durna); iStockphoto (48b/paul kline); Safababy.com (49/Safababy Ltd); iStockphoto (50/Gert Vrey); iStockphoto (52/jo unruh); iStockphoto (53tl/Ethan Myerson); iStockphoto (53tr/Jacek Chabraszewski); iStockphoto (53bl/Phil Date); iStockphoto (53br/Rosemarie Gearhart); iStockphoto (54t/René Jansa); iStockphoto (54ct/Jani Bryson); iStockphoto (54cb/Yvonne Chamberlain); iStockphoto (54b/onebluelight); iStockphoto (55t/Grafissimo); iStockphoto (55c/Diane Diederich); Alamy (55b/mainpicture); Alamy (56t/Petr Bonek); iStockphoto (56b/Arjan de Jager); iStockphoto (57t/Vanessa Morosini); Alamy (57c/Blend Images); iStockphoto (57b/Susan H. Smith); iStockphoto (60/Ekaterina Monakhova); iStockphoto (61/Plus); iStockphoto (62/Mikhail Kokhanchikov); iStockphoto (63/AVAVA); iStockphoto (64/Robert Dant); iStockphoto (65/Ekaterina Monakhova); iStockphoto (66/Yulya Shilova); iStockphoto (72l/thumb); iStockphoto (72c/pablo del rio sotelo); iStockphoto (72r/Charles Brutlag); iStockphoto (73/dasha2021); Rex Features (75t/Voisin/Phanie); British Toy and Hobby Association (75b); iStockphoto (77/Jaroslaw Grubba); iStockphoto (78/Semen Barkovskiy); iStockphoto (79/ kkgas); iStockphoto (80t/Floortje); iStockphoto (80ct/Alasdair Thomson); Alamy (80cb/Inspirestock Inc.); Philips Avent (80b); iStockphoto (82/David Hernandez); iStockphoto (83t/Elena Schweitzer); iStockphoto (83c/Jenny Horne); iStockphoto (83b/Paul Johnson); iStockphoto (84/AVAVA); iStockphoto (86/Oleg Kozlov); Food Standards Agency (88/© Crown copyright material is reproduced with the permission of the Controller of HMSO and Queen's Printer for Scotland.); Rex Features (88); iStockphoto (89/Nagy-Bagoly Ilona); Alamy (90t/Bubbles Photolibrary); iStockphoto (90b/Jillian Pond); iStockphoto (92/Wojciech Gajda); iStockphoto (93/Matauw); iStockphoto (97/Greg Brookes); iStockphoto (98/vladimir kondrachov); iStockphoto (100/dagmar heymans); iStockphoto (101t/Alexia Bannister); iStockphoto (101c/Tom Hahn); iStockphoto (101b/Brad Killer); iStockphoto (103/Gerville Hall); iStockphoto (105/Monika Adamczyk); iStockphoto (108/Zsolt Nyulaszi); iStockphoto (109/Teresa Guerrero); iStockphoto (110t/Wendy Shiao); iStockphoto (110b/Christopher Futcher); iStockphoto (119/Sarah Howling); iStockphoto (125/Fertnig); iStockphoto (128/Alena Yakusheva); iStockphoto (129/Ekaterina Monakhova); iStockphoto (130t/Stanislav Fridkin); Rex Features (130b/Image Source); British Toy and Hobby Association (131l); Rex Features (131r/Voisin/Phanie); Alamy (133/Sally and Richard Greenhill); Alamy (134/david hancock); iStockphoto (137/morganl); iStockphoto (138/jo unruh); iStockphoto (141/Steve Cole); iStockphoto (144/Kim Gunkel); Rex Features (148/Stuart Clarke); Corbis (153/ David H. Wells); iStockphoto (155/andres balcazar).

Introduction

This aim of this book is to help you develop the knowledge and understanding you will need to complete the OCR GCSE in Home Economics (Child Development) course.

Your tutor will create a learning programme that gives you opportunities to explore a wide range of child development topics and which will prepare you for your assessments. This book provides coverage of all of the topics in the OCR GCSE Home Economics (Child Development) specification and a range of questions and activities that will help you to develop your understanding of the needs of young children and the factors that influence their development in contemporary society.

Each chapter in this book covers one part of the OCR GCSE Home Economics (Child Development) specification. The chapters provide you with opportunities to

▶ develop your knowledge of children's needs and patterns of development

▶ increase your understanding of how children can be and are provided with different forms of care to enable them to develop appropriately

▶ develop your critical thinking skills as well as your writing abilities through work on case studies, activities and end-of-topic questions

▶ develop the knowledge and understanding you will need to successfully complete assignments and cover the assessment criteria that are part of the OCR GCSE Home Economics (Child Development) award.

Features of the book

The book closely follows the specification (syllabus) of the OCR GCSE Home Economics (Child Development) award. This means that all of the topics and issues referred to in the course specification are fully covered. You will find the following features in the book:

▶ **Chapter introduction** – this is a short, introductory section at the start of each chapter that tells you what the chapter is going to focus on.

▶ **Key terms** – the main ideas (concepts) and the language of child development are briefly explained in this feature. Key terms are also highlighted in the text itself.

▶ **Over to you!** – these are short activities that aim to get you thinking about an issue or topic. They can usually be completed on the spot without doing any more research.

▶ **Activities** – these are designed to extend your knowledge and understanding by encouraging you to find out a bit more about a topic or issue you have been learning about.

▶ **Case study** – these are short examples of situations and stories from the world of child development and child care. They encourage you to apply your knowledge and understanding to realistic situations that you might face in child care situations.

▶ **Topic check** – this is a list of questions about the topic you have been studying. You should try to answer as many of these as you can.

Assessment

The OCR GCSE Home Economics (Child Development) award is assessed through Controlled Assessment (a Child Study and Short Tasks assignments) and a written examination. The controlled assessment work contributes 60% of your overall marks, while the examination contributes the remaining 40%.

We have tried to write a book that will helps you to gain a good, clear understanding of a range of child development and child care topics. The case study and activity focus of the book also aims to give you an insight into what it is like to care for children, as a parent and child care worker. Taking a child development course should enable you to think about both the theory and practice of children's development. It is hoped that this will encourage you to provide thoughtful, supportive and safe care for children in the future.

Good luck with your course!

Janet Stearns and Mark Walsh

1 Family and parenting

Introduction

This chapter is divided into four topics:

1.1 Family structures and change

1.2 Children in care

1.3 Pre-conceptual health and care

1.4 Methods of contraception

Overall, this chapter introduces you to a range of topics and issues relating to the family and parenting. Topic 1.1 describes different types of family structure and relationships in families, and considers how the family influences child development. There may be circumstances where a child is unable to live with their own family, either temporarily or permanently. Topic 1.2 outlines different forms of provision for children in care and considers reasons why alternative families or local authority provision are sometimes required for children in this situation. Topic 1.3 outlines a wide range of

factors that affect the decision to have children, and the roles and responsibilities of parenthood. Topic 1.4 describes and evaluates methods of contraception, their efficiency and reliability.

By the end of this chapter you should be able to recognise and understand:

▶ that there is a range of different family types in UK society

▶ why there are changing patterns in parenting and family life

▶ the reasons why children may be in local authority care

▶ that the decision to have children is affected by a range of factors and that parenthood has a big impact on an individual's role and responsibilities in life

▶ that there are a number of different methods of contraception, with varying degrees of efficiency and reliability.

Family structures and change

▶ Getting started

This topic focuses on the ways families can be organised and the reasons why family structures have changed over time. When you have completed this topic you should:

- know about different forms of family structure in Britain
- be able to describe factors that influence changes in family structure.

🔑 Key terms

Blended family: a form of step-family in which one or both partners have children from previous relationships

Cohabit: live together

Extended family: a family that includes parents, children and other relatives (e.g. grandparents, uncles, aunts)

Life events: major events in a person's life that affect their development and wellbeing

Nuclear family: two adult parents and their children

One-parent family: a family consisting of a lone parent and at least one dependent child

Socialisation: the process of teaching (and learning) the attitudes, values and expectations of society

Stigma: a characteristic, behaviour or label that discredits or damages the reputation of a person

Family structures

A family is a group of people who live together or who are related by blood ties, marriage or adoption. A family usually consists of one or more parents and at least one child. The classic, popular image of the family is of a married couple and two children. However, family structures in the United Kingdom are much more diverse than this (see Figure 1.1). For example, a couple who **cohabit**, their children and any other relatives living with them also count as a 'family'. Regardless of the diverse ways in which it can be structured or organised, the family is seen as the basic building block of society because it performs a number of important functions.

The functions of the family

The modern family performs a number of important functions for its members. These include:

▶ providing physical resources (like food, shelter and clothing) for the healthy growth and development of children

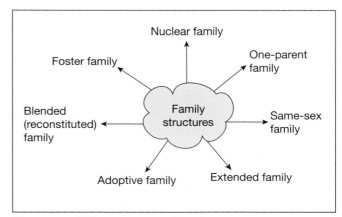

Figure 1.1 Different types of family structure

- physical and psychological protection of family members
- the primary **socialisation** of children
- providing love and emotional support
- providing opportunities for learning and development.

The family has the basic task of meeting the needs of its members. The needs of each individual within a family will differ and change in response to their:

- life stage
- pattern of growth and development
- experience of health problems, and social or emotional development issues
- cultural background.

Each of the different types of family structure that exist can perform these functions and can provide the conditions needed for a child's development if the family is cohesive, supportive and stable.

Socialisation

Teaching children how to behave in society is a key part of the family's role. Children need to learn appropriate attitudes and values and how to behave in different situations. As a result, parents have a lot of responsibility for bringing up children 'properly'. You may have noticed newspaper and television news stories that blame some families for the negative and antisocial behaviour of their children. Parents need to be role models, guiding and supporting children's development. It is important to note that a child's upbringing will affect their own approach to parenting if they go on to have children themselves.

Figure 1.2 Types of family structure

Family structure	Key characteristics
Nuclear family	Two heterosexual parents and dependent child(ren)
Extended family	Nuclear family plus additional relatives living together
One-parent family	Single parent and dependent child
Blended family	Two parents with dependent children from previous relationships and/or their own child(ren)
Same-sex family	Two gay or lesbian parents and dependent child(ren)
Adoptive family	Any form of family with one or more adopted children
Foster family	Any form of family with one or more fostered children

Activity

Imagine that you have a child. You (and your partner) are now responsible for bringing the child up. What kinds of things do you need to teach your child before they go to school? Make a list of the things a child needs to learn about:

- behaviour
- relationships
- communication
- manners.

Compare your list with those of a couple of class colleagues and share ideas about your priorities

Nuclear families

A **nuclear family** is based around two heterosexual parents and their dependent children living together in the same household. A nuclear family tends to have some contact with other relatives who may also live in nuclear families but not in the same household. Though they have family connections to other relatives, nuclear families tend to be seen as independent, self-sufficient units. This doesn't mean that the parents in a nuclear family will necessarily provide all of the childcare they need. Some nuclear families use childminders, grandparents or other childcare services to look after their children while they are at work, for example. However, on the whole, the parents do have the main responsibility and spend most time caring for their children.

Extended families

Extended families are nuclear families that are extended by the presence of grandparents or other relatives living in the same household as part of a single family unit. Extended families were much more common in the UK in the 19th and early 20th centuries. However, a range of social changes in the 20th century led to their general decline and the growth of the nuclear family. Despite this, extended families are still present in the UK, particularly in South Asian, Chinese and some other minority ethnic communities. One of the benefits of living in an extended family for children (and parents) is that there are more adults around to provide assistance with day-to-day activities and childcare needs.

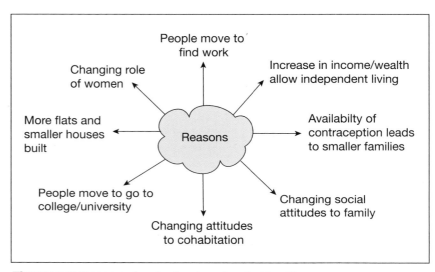

Figure 1.3 Reasons for decline in extended families

One-parent families

The **one-parent family** is one of the fastest growing, though not the most common, type of family structure in the UK. It consists of a single parent (usually the mother) and at least one dependent child. The parent living with the child may share custody and responsibility for childcare with the child's other parent. Though it is not always the case, many one-parent families have previously been part of a nuclear or extended family. Separation, divorce or the death of one partner may be the reason why a one-parent family is formed. Changes in social attitudes, particularly a decline in the **stigma** associated with being an 'unmarried mother', have made one-parent families and the birth of children outside of marriage more socially acceptable.

 Over to you!

How do you think people view 'single parents'? In your opinion, has the stigma associated with being part of a one-parent family changed? What are your own thoughts about the impact that having only one parent at home has on children's development?

Blended families

Blended families are also known as step-families and reconstituted families. They are families that have been (re)formed, usually from pre-existing one-parent or nuclear families. In some blended families, both parents bring children from previous relationships. In other cases only one parent already has children and the new couple may have children of their own. As a result, these families consist of a blend of different types of relationships in which individuals can be biologically related or step-children and half-brothers or sisters.

Same-sex families

These relatively new, contemporary families consist of same-sex partners living with dependent children who may be their own offspring, adopted or fostered. In a similar way to one-parent and blended families, same-sex families are sometimes formed from pre-existing nuclear or one-parent families. Same-sex families with two parents are a form of nuclear family.

Adoptive families

An adoptive family is a family that has an adopted child living within it. This can be any type of family structure but will always include at least one child who has been legally adopted by the parents.

Foster families

Like adoptive families, foster families are usually pre-existing families where the parents take on temporary fostering responsibility for a child who is unable to live in their own family. In many cases the fostered child will return home, though some children are adopted and live with the family permanently or move to live within a residential care home for children and young people.

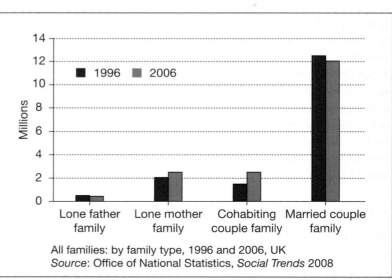

All families: by family type, 1996 and 2006, UK
Source: Office of National Statistics, *Social Trends* 2008

Figure 1.4 Prevalence of different family structures in the UK

Activity

Look at Figure 1.4 showing how common four different types of family structure are in the UK.

1. Which type of family was the most common in 2006?

2. Which type of family structure was the most unusual in 2006?

3. Approximately how many one-parent families were there in the UK in 2006?

4. Which type of family structure increased most between 1996 and 2006?

Reasons for family diversity

Family structures have changed over time in the UK. The family is now much more diverse than it was 100, 50 or even 25 years ago. Family diversity is the result of a number of social changes that have affected wider UK society. These include:

▶ There has been a growth in the multicultural population, with different ethnic communities introducing their own traditions and forms of family life. People with south Asian and east African heritage, for example, tend to live in extended families. This often involves three generations living in the same household and a greater role for grandparents and other relatives in everyday family life.

▶ Attitudes to marriage and divorce have changed since the late 1960s. Changes in divorce laws since the late 1960s have made divorce much easier. This has had an impact on family structures as people have ended marriages and begun new relationships that may involve cohabitation or remarriage.

▶ Changes in attitudes to sexuality have enabled same-sex couples to adopt, foster and conceive their own children.

▶ There have been changes in the availability of contraception and sexual health education. These have given people knowledge and the ability to control when they have children and how many they have. One result has been a reduction in the size of families.

▶ Changes in lifestyle have allowed couples to marry and have children at an older age and share childcare and domestic responsibilities differently from their parents.

▶ Changing patterns of work and geographical mobility since the 1980s and 1990s have led to more people moving away from where they grew up to find work, as well as more women in the workforce. The need and demand for childcare services has grown as a result of these changes.

▶ Changes in reproductive technology have enabled couples with fertility problems, same-sex couples and single people to have children where they haven't been able to conceive naturally.

▶ Changes in the social welfare system have provided more support for families and have targeted support for low-income, particularly one-parent, families. This has enabled more nuclear and one-parent families to live independently of other relatives.

Activity

Using what you have learnt about the reasons for family diversity, and any additional ideas you might have about this, produce a poster or leaflet that summarises the reasons why there is now a range of different types of family in the UK.

Changing roles and responsibilities in the family

The traditional image of the family is based on the idea of a relatively strong and clear 'sexual division of labour'. This involved the man going out to work to earn the money the family needed while the woman stayed at home as mother and housewife. In this traditional arrangement, the woman's domestic role was to care for the children, her husband and the house. This traditional sexual division of labour is much less common in the UK today.

In contemporary UK society, a woman is still more likely to take on the childcare and domestic responsibilities in the home than her male partner or husband. However, modern-day fathers are also now much more likely to be involved in looking after the home and caring for their children than their own fathers were. Today, couples tend to see the domestic and childcare aspects of family life as more of a shared responsibility than in the past. The balance of responsibilities in the home has changed as women's roles in wider society and people's expectations of their relationships have changed. Women now want to and are expected to go out to work so that they can contribute economically, and fathers are more likely to want greater involvement and better relationships with their children.

Where both parents work, a family may benefit from:

- a better standard of living due to the higher income being earned
- fathers having better relationships with their children due to sharing of childcare responsibilities
- children learning that family life is based around shared responsibilities.

Changing family relationships

Relationships and roles within a family change as the individuals who make up the family grow, develop and change as people. The circumstances a family lives in can also change as a result of both positive and negative **life events**. Divorce, remarriage, unemployment, the birth of children, changing job or career and the experience of disability, illness or even a death within a family, can all affect the roles, relationships and behaviour of those living within a family.

Over to you!

What kind of relationship would you like to have with your partner if you have a family in the future? Will you be happy with a traditional 'sexual division of labour' and clear-cut woman/housewife, man/worker roles, or will you insist on a different balance and sharing of family responsibilities?

Case study

Egil Johnsen, aged 38, has recently moved from Norway to live with Joanna, aged 35, and her daughter Eve, aged 3. Joanna and Egil are expecting their first child together in 3 months' time. They have decided to get married and live in the UK near to Joanna's parents and her sister. Joanna thinks that she will need help and support from other members of her family when the baby is born. Egil is happy to move to the UK but says he will miss his brother and sister who live in Norway. He is also going to miss his daughter, Anna, who lives with his former wife, Erica, and her new partner. Egil is excited about 'this new kind of family life' but also admits it makes his life quite complicated.

1. What kind of family structure will Egil, Joanna, Eve and their new baby live in?

2. Identify the people who are members of Joanna's extended family.

3. Explain how the case study illustrates the diverse range of family structures in the UK.

Topic check

1. Identify five different types of family and their main characteristics.
2. How is a nuclear family different from an extended family?
3. Describe the qualities a family needs to provide appropriate conditions for a child's development.
4. Explain why there is now a diverse range of family types in the UK.
5. Describe how roles and responsibilities within the family have changed over the last 30 years.
6. Identify examples of factors that can cause relationships to change within a family.

Children in care

This topic focuses on the types of care provided for children who are unable to live with their own family, either temporarily or permanently. When you have completed this topic you should:

- be able to identify reasons why children are sometimes looked after outside of their own family
- understand what fostering and adoption involve and the differences between them.

 Key terms

Adoption: the legal process of placing a child with non-birth parent or parents

Fostering: the provision of temporary care for a child unable to live with their own parent(s)

Institutionalising: placing a person in an institution

Local authority: a council

Respite care: care that provides short-term, temporary relief to those caring for children or other relatives

Children in care

Children who are unable to live with their birth or adoptive families, or other relatives, are usually looked after by **local authorities**. Local authorities throughout the UK provide residential care homes for looked after children but try to avoid placing children in them for long periods of time. Where children have to be looked after outside of their own family for a period of time, most agencies try to work with the child's parents and return them home or find the child a temporary or permanent foster family.

Children are sometimes unable to live with their family because:

- they have special needs and the child's parents need a temporary **respite care** break
- their parent(s) are unable to care for them because of serious or ongoing illness or social problems
- their parent is in prison
- they have been orphaned and have no other relatives willing or able to look after them
- they have been neglected or rejected by their parents

▶ they have been abused in some way

▶ their parents are incapable of providing adequate care for them.

A child who is thought to be 'at risk' of abuse or neglect within their family can be removed by a local authority that obtains a court order. A family could also make a voluntary application to the court for their children to be taken into care if they are unable to look after them. In all cases where a child is looked after by the local authority, they will be allocated a specialist social worker. This person is responsible for arranging and monitoring their care and for working with the child to plan for their future. Despite the best efforts of local authority social workers, foster carers and residential care staff, children who are taken into care often feel lonely and scared, and are emotionally distressed when it becomes clear that they are being taken into care.

Over to you!

How might both a child with complex disabilities and her parents benefit from her receiving regular, respite foster care?

Residential care for children

Most residential care for children is provided by local authorities. However, private, voluntary sector and local authority residential homes all exist in the UK and are an important source of supported, usually short-term, care for children.

The number of residential care homes for children has reduced significantly since the 1960s and 1970s. This is partly due to the realisation that foster care provides better opportunities for children in care to develop as individuals and experience family life. However, it has also been recognised that standards of care for children in residential care homes has been variable (sometimes good, sometimes poor) and in some cases has led to children being abused by care staff and other children. A number of investigations into residential childcare that were carried out in the 1980s and 1990s revealed abuse scandals dating back many years. Research into the lives and experiences of children in care has also shown that their educational attainments are poorer, their risk of homelessness higher on leaving care and that they are more at risk of developing mental health problems than children cared for in families. As a result, efforts have been made to improve standards of provision, and children living in residential care today are given greater support and protection than in the past.

Residential childcare services are still provided and used throughout the UK because:

▶ they are a way of providing vulnerable and 'at risk' children with a professional level of care

▶ they offer an effective way of meeting a vulnerable child's basic and security needs in often difficult circumstances

▶ they can provide short-term, temporary respite for both a child and their parents when problems develop within a family

▶ they offer children a source of immediate, secure care and a place of safety if they are removed from their family by court order or if their parents are suddenly unable to care for them.

The main disadvantages of residential care homes are that:

▶ they are, despite the efforts of staff, institutional environments with shared facilities

▶ children must conform to the rules and regulations of the care home (which will be different from the more informal 'rules' most children have at home)

▶ children living in residential care will not experience the important physical and emotional bonding with parents that children living in a family will experience

▶ some children remain vulnerable to exploitation and abuse by others within and from outside the home.

Residential care homes for children try to overcome some of the disadvantages associated with this type of care by developing a family-like structure and atmosphere. This is usually based around adult care staff taking responsibility for small groups of children and each child having a close relationship with a named care worker. Some children benefit from this because it gives them an experience of supported, structured and secure care, which they may not have had before. Despite this, local authorities will generally try to find a child a foster placement before placing them in residential care for any length of time.

Foster care

This involves placing a child with a family who will provide care and support on a temporary basis. The child is treated as part of the family. Children who are fostered often feel emotionally vulnerable and can have challenging behaviour. Foster carers must enjoy looking after children, be resilient and prepared to be very supportive. However, a foster carer doesn't assume parental rights. The local authority becomes the child's legal guardian.

 Over to you!

What impact (positive and negative) do you think that fostering a child might have on a family? How do you think you would have reacted if your parent(s) had fostered a child when you were growing up?

Children can be placed for short- or long-term **fostering**, depending on the individual circumstances of the child. Some children who are fostered go on to be adopted by the family they are placed with. The different types of foster care are described in Figure 1.5. Each type of foster care arrangement is designed to meet the varying needs of children in care.

Figure 1.5 Types of foster care

Type of foster care	What does it involve?
Permanent (long-term) fostering	Foster family cares for the child until they reach 18 years of age. This is an alternative to adoption where the child has a strong bond with their birth family but is unable to live with them.
Emergency foster care	This usually involves providing care for a child who needs somewhere safe to stay for a few days or nights.
Short-term foster care	The foster family provides care for a few weeks or months while plans are made for the child's future placement or return home.
Respite foster care	Children who live with their own family or with other foster carers are placed in another foster family to give their usual carers a break (respite). This is typically used for children with special needs or behavioural difficulties. It is also known as 'family link' and 'shared care'.
Remand foster care	This is provided for young people who are 'remanded' by the courts in England and Wales into local authority care or placed in foster care as an alternative to secure accommodation by a Scottish court.
Family and friends (kinship) foster care	Kinship care involves children being cared for by relatives or friends of their parents whom they already know. It may still be arranged and monitored by the local authority.
Parent and child fostering	This involves carers looking after a parent and child(ren) while they prepare for a more independent future.
Private fostering	This happens where parents make private arrangements for their child to be cared for by people they are not related to. The carers have no parental responsibilities. If the child is under 16 years of age (or 18 if disabled) the local authority has to be informed and will monitor the arrangements to safeguard the child's welfare.

Foster care is thought to be a better option than residential care because:

▶ it avoids **institutionalising** the child and promotes their individual development in a family context

▶ it gives the child the experience of living in a supportive family structure

▶ it provides the child with opportunities to develop the skills needed for supportive family relationships

▶ foster care can be more focused, flexible and individualised to meet the child's needs than the more impersonal care provided in larger residential settings.

However, foster care can also lead to problems for some children because:

▶ they are more isolated than in a residential childcare setting

▶ families can be difficult to inspect and monitor

▶ they are less likely to complain about their treatment than they are in residential care homes.

Foster carers are assessed and monitored for their suitability by the local authority. They must comply with the requirements of the Children Act (1989). For example, they must:

▶ allow access to natural parents if in a child's best interests

▶ bring up the child in their own religion

▶ provide the same standard of care as for their own children

▶ return the child to the local authority when required to do so.

Case study

Colin and Sara are long-term foster carers. They live with their birth son Dan and foster child Jonny. Dan is 14 and still at school. Jonny is now 16 and has just started college. Colin and Sara have a close bond with Jonny. They have looked after him since he was 3 years old. They say that they treat him the same way as they treat their own son, Dan. Sara said that 'he's part of our family, we love him. Even if he left home we'd stay in close touch. He knows he's part of our family.' Jonny still sees his own mum every few months and says he's just got 'extra parents' but that they all get on. He has always been happy living with Colin and Sara and considers Dan to be his brother.

1. What type of foster care arrangements are being described in the case study?

2. How might Jonny have benefited from being placed in this foster family?

3. Why do you think people like Colin and Sara become foster parents?

Adoption

Adoption involves a legal process where an adult, or often a couple, become the parents of children they have not given birth to. Unlike fostering, adoptive parents have full legal rights and responsibilities for the child. In a positive way, adoption can give a child:

▶ a sense of belonging and being wanted

▶ a settled family life within a family home.

Children who are looked after in residential homes and in foster families can live less secure and more unsettled lives because they are sometimes moved between care homes and foster carers. This can be emotionally upsetting, disruptive to their education and emotional development, and leave them feeling unwanted and uncared for.

Activity

Using the internet, find out about the experience of fostering and adoption by visiting the following websites:

www.bemyparent.org.uk

www.baaf.org.uk

www.thefca.co.uk

You can compare modern-day experiences of being a child in care with those of children in the past by visiting www.hiddenlives.org.uk.

Couples who want to adopt a child must first approach an adoption agency. This is usually a local authority, though there are also voluntary and private sector adoption agencies. It is possible to adopt a baby or child of any age, though there was a preference for adopting babies and toddlers in the past. However, social changes have led to more older children being available for adoption in recent times. People who wish to adopt children generally do so as a way of forming or extending a family.

Figure 1.6 Differences between adoption and fostering

Fostering	Adoption
Foster parents have no legal rights over the child.	Adoptive parents have full legal rights over the child.
Foster parents receive an allowance from the fostering agency to cover the costs of caring for the child.	Adoptive parents have personal responsibility for paying the costs of caring for the child.
Foster carers have temporary responsibility for the child.	Adoptive parents have permanent responsibility for the child.
Foster carers are monitored and supported by the local authority.	Adoptive parents only receive monitoring and support where significant childcare problems arise.

✔ **Topic check**

1 Who usually takes on legal responsibility for looking after children in care?
2 Give three reasons why children are sometimes unable to live with their own families and are taken into care.
3 Describe what fostering and adoption involve and explain the main differences between them.
4 What are the advantages and disadvantages of local authority residential care homes for children in care?
5 Explain why fostering and adoption are thought to be better for children in care than placements in residential children's homes.
6 Explain why a couple may wish to adopt a child and what they would have to do to achieve this.

Pre-conceptual health and care

▶ Getting started

This topic is about making the decision to have a baby and how important it is to prepare for parenthood. On completion of this topic you should:

- know the factors a couple need to think about in preparation for becoming parents
- understand the importance of being healthy before deciding to become pregnant
- be able to describe lifestyle choices and medical factors that can influence pre-conceptual health.

Key terms

Folic acid: also known as folate and vitamin B9, this is a B vitamin that is essential for cell growth and reproduction

Genetic counselling: information and support provided by a specialist counsellor to people who are concerned about the possibility of transmitting

birth abnormalities or genetic conditions to their offspring

Pre-conceptual: before conception

Rubella: a contagious virus also known as 'German measles' that can cause a miscarriage or serious birth defects if caught during pregnancy

Being a parent

The decision to have a baby is one of the most important choices a couple will ever make. Being a parent is a very responsible job and should always be considered carefully. There are many factors that can influence the decision to have a baby. The most important consideration is that the new baby should be welcomed into a loving, caring family and a nurturing environment. Parenthood has a major impact on a couple's relationship and adds a new dimension to their lifestyle. There may be practical and financial issues to think about too, like whether the couple will have enough money or need to move to a bigger house. There will also be other considerations, such as whether the couple's relationship is secure enough to cope with the responsibility of caring for a baby, changes to their social life and dealing with sleepless nights!

Pre-conceptual care

Pre-conceptual care refers to the care that should be taken both physically, socially and emotionally before deciding to become pregnant. This includes lifestyle factors like eating healthily and not being overweight, taking regular exercise and not smoking or drinking alcohol. It also includes medical factors like avoiding contact with infectious diseases and having a check-up at the doctors. It is important to make sure that the woman is immune to **rubella**, which can cause

The impact of parenthood on lifestyle

abnormalities to the unborn baby if the mother becomes infected during pregnancy.

Women who are planning to become pregnant are also advised to take **folic acid**, which is one of the B group of vitamins. Folic acid is found in foods like whole grains and nuts and can also be taken in tablet form as a supplement. Research has shown that folic acid can help to prevent conditions like spina bifida (an abnormality in the development of the brain and spinal cord).

Some women may need more specific tests before deciding to become pregnant, particularly if there is a family history of certain medical conditions. This would be investigated through **genetic counselling** to check for inherited conditions through routine checks and blood tests.

 Activity

Using the internet and other sources, investigate the causes, symptoms and effects of rubella. Use your findings to produce a poster or leaflet that informs women about rubella and that encourages them to have their immunisation status checked.

 Case study

Aja and Ryan have been married for 2 years. Aja is 25 years old and works full time as a receptionist at the local health centre. Ryan is 26 years old and works as an engineer for a construction company. Aja describes her ethnicity as black British and Ryan is white European. They currently rent a one-bedroom flat, which has no garden, but is close to a large park. Aja walks to work every day and Ryan takes the bus. They do not own a car. They have decided that they would like to have a baby and are making preparations for Aja's pregnancy.

1. What are the positive factors about Aja and Ryan deciding to become parents?

2. What are the possible negative factors?

3. Can you give examples of some of the decisions and choices that Aja and Ryan may have to make before trying to have a baby?

Figure 1.7 Examples of inherited conditions

Cystic fibrosis	A condition that produces thick mucus in the lungs and causes breathing difficulties
Haemophilia	A condition that reduces the ability of the blood to clot
Sickle cell anaemia	A blood disorder that causes abnormal red blood cells
Phenylketonuria (PKU)	A condition that affects the ability to digest protein, which can lead to brain damage if not treated
Muscular dystrophy	A condition that causes muscle weakness

Activity

Use the internet, library or other resources to investigate 'genetic inheritance' and how specific characteristics and medical conditions, like cystic fibrosis and haemophilia, can be inherited by children from their parents. Make a presentation of your findings to your class colleagues.

Children inherit genes from both parents. These genes determine certain characteristics like hair colour and blood group. Some genes also carry defects that may cause inherited disorders. The risk is greater for couples with a family history of inherited conditions, although some disorders can happen  completely out of the blue. It is important to remember that most babies are born healthy and inherited conditions are rare. Genetic counselling will help couples to understand the possible risks and to make their own decisions.

Over to you!

Which of your personal characteristics do you think you have inherited from your parents? Make a list of these and compare it with the list of a class colleague.

Case study

Aja and Ryan have made some important decisions in preparation for Aja's pregnancy. Ryan has given up smoking and Aja, who is a vegetarian, is making sure that she is eating healthily with lots of fruit and vegetables in her diet. She continues to exercise regularly, walking to work every day and swimming every week. Ryan has been to the local library and taken out some books about preparation for fatherhood, pregnancy and birth.

1. What positive pre-conceptual decisions have Aja and Ryan made?

2. Can you think of any other decisions that Aja and Ryan might make as part of their pre-conceptual health and care?

3. Suggest two ways in which Aja and Ryan's lifestyle may change if they are successful in becoming parents.

Topic check

1 Why is it important to plan the right time to start a family?

2 What do you understand by the term 'pre-conceptual care'?

3 Describe some of the lifestyle decisions a couple may need to make before becoming pregnant.

4 Why is it important to check a woman's immunity to rubella (German measles) as part of pre-conceptual care?

5 Why is folic acid important as part of pre-conceptual care?

6 Explain what is meant by genetic counselling.

Topic 1.4
Methods of contraception

 Getting started

This topic focuses on the importance of planning to have a family and the different choices of contraception methods. On completion of this topic you should:

■ know about different methods of contraception, their reliability and how they work

■ be able to describe the advantages and disadvantages of different contraception methods

■ be able to discuss the factors that might influence the choice of contraception method used.

 Key terms

Barrier methods: contraceptives that prevent the sperm from reaching the egg and protect against sexually transmitted infections

Cervix: the neck of the uterus (womb)

Contraception: the use of birth control methods to prevent pregnancy

Gonorrhoea: a sexually transmitted infection

HIV: human immunodeficiency virus (which can cause acquired immune deficiency syndrome (AIDS))

Hormones: chemical substances created by glands in the body

Oestrogen: a female hormone produced by the ovaries

Ovulation: the release of an ovum from the ovary

Progestogen: a form of the female hormone progesterone used in contraceptive pills

Uterus: a major organ of the female reproductive system, also called the womb

Family planning

Part of the decision-making process in choosing to have a baby is about the use of **contraception**. Planning to have a family is very important because couples need to make sure that they are ready to take on the responsibility of a baby, practically, emotionally and financially.

There are many different methods of contraception for both men and women and some are more effective and reliable than others. Some of the more reliable methods include:

▶ condoms (98% effective)

▶ contraceptive pills (99% effective)

▶ male or female sterilisation (99% effective).

Natural methods of contraception

Natural methods of contraception do not require any medical advice or artificial aids. This means that they have no side effects and are acceptable to all religions and cultures.

18

There are two main methods of contraception:

▶ Abstention (not having sexual intercourse) – this is the only completely reliable method of contraception (100% effective).

▶ Natural family planning (fertility awareness) – this method relies on understanding when the woman is at the most fertile time in her menstrual cycle (usually during **ovulation**). Sexual intercourse is avoided during this time and therefore it is unlikely that pregnancy will occur. However, some women's menstrual cycles are unpredictable and it can therefore be difficult to calculate the exact timing.

Barrier methods of contraception

Barrier methods of contraception work by creating an artificial barrier that prevents the male sperm coming into contact with the female ovum (egg). An advantage of some barrier methods of contraception, such as male condoms, is that they help to prevent sexually transmitted infections (STIs) such as human immunodeficiency virus (**HIV**) and **gonorrhoea**. They must be used correctly in order to be effective.

There are a number of barrier contraceptive devices available, including those discussed below.

Male condoms

Male condoms are widely available and free at many family planning clinics. They are made of latex rubber and are designed to fit over the erect penis during sexual intercourse. At ejaculation, sperm are trapped in the specially designed tip of the condom and are therefore prevented from entering the woman's vagina.

Female condoms (e.g. Femidom)

Female condoms are widely available and free at many family planning clinics. They are made of soft rubber and fit like a sleeve inside the vagina, therefore preventing sperm from entering.

Diaphragm (cap)

The female diaphragm is a dome-shaped device made of flexible rubber. It is designed to fit over the woman's **cervix** (neck of the womb) and must be specially measured and fitted by a doctor. The woman will be taught how to put in and take out the diaphragm by herself. It should be used with spermicidal cream or gel (which kills sperm). A diaphragm works by preventing sperm from entering the woman's **uterus** (womb) and it must be left in place for at least six hours after sexual intercourse.

Female-only methods of contraception

Female-only methods of contraception include:

▶ contraceptive pills

▶ contraceptive injections and implants

▶ intrauterine devices and systems.

All these methods need medical advice and supervision. Some also carry a risk of side effects like irregular periods and weight gain.

Activity

Use the internet, library or other resources to investigate sexually transmitted infections. Design a leaflet or web page for teenagers with the main facts about common sexually transmitted infections, how they can be prevented and where to get information and advice.

Combined pill

The combined contraceptive pill contains two **hormones**, **oestrogen** and **progestogen**. It works by preventing ovulation, and therefore no ova (eggs) are released for possible fertilisation. The combined pill must be taken as directed and is not suitable for women who smoke as this can increase the risk of blood clots.

Progestogen-only pill (mini-pill)

The mini-pill contains the hormone progestogen, which causes changes in the woman's uterus and cervix. This makes it very difficult for sperm to fertilise the ovum.

Contraceptive injections and implants

Contraceptive injections and implants contain the hormone progestogen, which is released into the woman's body and prevents ovulation. The contraceptive implant is a small, plastic tube, which is inserted under the skin of the woman's upper arm. It can be effective for up to 5 years. Contraceptive injections are usually given every 12 weeks.

Intrauterine devices (IUD, coil or loop) and systems (IUS)

Intrauterine devices and systems are small, plastic appliances that are fitted into the woman's uterus by a doctor. They work by preventing implantation of a fertilised ovum in the uterus and can stay in place for 3 to 10 years, depending on the type used. Women are taught how to check regularly that the device is in the correct place.

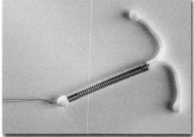

An IUD

Emergency contraception

The most widely used method of emergency contraception is the 'morning after' pill. These pills can prevent a fertilised ovum from implanting in the uterus, but must be taken within 72 hours of sexual intercourse taking place. This method of contraception is only suitable for use in an emergency, where unprotected sexual intercourse has taken place or a contraception method has failed.

Permanent contraception

Conception can be permanently prevented by the procedure of either male or female sterilisation. This decision should always be considered carefully, as in most cases it will mean that the sterilised partner is no longer fertile. It is a choice often made by couples who have completed their family and decided that they do not want any more children.

Male sterilisation (vasectomy)

A vasectomy is a relatively straightforward surgical procedure that involves cutting the vas deferens (sperm ducts), which prevents sperm making their journey from the testes. This means there are no sperm in the semen that is ejaculated.

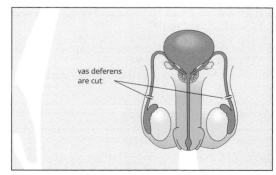

vas deferens are cut

Figure 1.8 Male sterilisation

In very rare cases, this procedure can be reversed, but in general, it should be considered permanent.

Female sterilisation

This is a surgical procedure performed under general anaesthetic. The fallopian tubes are cut or sealed and this prevents the ova from making their journey to meet the sperm. The procedure is usually irreversible.

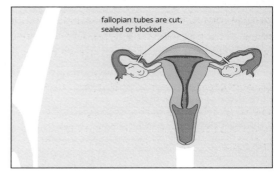

fallopian tubes are cut, sealed or blocked

Figure 1.9 Female sterilisation

Figure 1.10 Methods of contraception

Advantages	Disadvantages
Natural methods of contraception	
1. No chemicals or equipment needed 2. No side effects 3. Acceptable to all faith groups	1. Does not protect against STIs 2. Must time intercourse to avoid fertile periods 3. Often ineffective without training to learn techniques
Male condoms	
1. Protects against STIs including HIV 2. Widely available and free from family planning clinics 3. Men can take responsibility for contraception	1. Condoms can split or slip off 2. Sexual intercourse may be interrupted to put on the condom 3. The penis should be quickly withdrawn from the vagina after ejaculation
Female condoms	
1. Protects against STIs 2. Widely available and free from some family planning clinics 3. Can be inserted at any time before sexual intercourse	1. Care should be taken to ensure that the penis enters the condom and not between the condom and the vagina 2. Sexual intercourse may be interrupted to insert the condom 3. They can be expensive to buy
Combined pill	
1. More than 99% effective if used as instructed 2. Suitable for most healthy women who do not smoke 3. Can reduce period pain and pre-menstrual tension	1. Must be taken regularly and on time. It is not effective if taken more than 12 hours late. 2. Can cause serious side effects like blood clots 3. Vomiting, diarrhoea and some medicines may stop the pill from working
Progesterone-only pill	
1. Can be taken by women who are breastfeeding 2. Can be taken by older women	1. Needs to be taken at the same time every day 2. May cause periods to be irregular 3. Vomiting, diarrhoea and some medicines may stop the pill from working
Diaphragm with spermicide	
1. Can be inserted before sexual intercourse 2. May protect against some STIs 3. There are many different kinds available	1. Needs to be inserted correctly to fit over the cervix 2. Sexual intercourse may be interrupted to insert the diaphragm

Figure 1.10 Methods of contraception *continued*

Advantages	Disadvantages
Intrauterine device (IUD)	
1. Effective as soon as it inserted 2. Can stay in place for several years, therefore contraception does not have to be thought about	1. Can cause heavier bleeding and longer periods 2. Not suitable for women who have heavy periods
Intrauterine system (IUS)	
1. Effective as soon as it inserted 2. Can stay in place for several years, therefore contraception does not have to be thought about 3. Periods will usually be shorter with lighter bleeding	1. Periods can be irregular for the first few months 2. Can cause some minor side effects like breast tenderness
Contraceptive injection	
1. More than 99% effective 2. Generally effective for up to 12 weeks	1. Can cause periods to become irregular 2. May take over a year for periods to return to normal after stopping the injections 3. May be some side effects such as weight gain and headaches
Contraceptive implant	
1. More than 99% effective 2. Generally effective for 3 to 5 years (depending on the type used)	1. Can cause periods to become irregular 2. May be some side effects such as weight gain and headaches

Activity

Discuss the factors that might influence the choice of contraception method for:

- Karimah and Aamir who have been married for 15 years and have three children aged 12, 10 and 7 years old.

- Sarah and Kevin who have been married for a year and would like to have children eventually.

- Tracey who is 22 and divorced with two children aged 2 and 4 years old. She is going out with Latif whom she has just met.

- Kylie is 17 and is thinking about having sex with her boyfriend whom she has been seeing for 3 months.

Topic check

1. Describe two barrier methods of contraception.
2. What are the names of the hormones in the combined contraceptive pill?
3. How does an intrauterine device (IUD) work as a method of contraception?
4. Give two examples of sexually transmitted infections (STIs).
5. Explain the disadvantages of natural family planning.
6. Outline some of the factors that might influence an individual's choice of contraception method.

2 Preparation for pregnancy and birth

Introduction

This chapter is divided into four topics:

2.1 Reproduction

2.2 Pregnancy and antenatal provision

2.3 Preparation for the birth of the new baby

2.4 Postnatal care

This chapter describes the earliest stages of child development, from conception until birth, and the forms of care a woman requires during this time. Topic 2.1 describes the biological process of reproduction and also identifies some of the problems and possible solutions associated with infertility. Topic 2.2 outlines a range of issues associated with pregnancy, including diet, the role of different health professionals, the stages of foetal development, and the range of routine checks and specialised tests that are part of antenatal provision. Topic 2.3 focuses on preparation for birth, including the choices available for delivery, the stages of labour and the role of the father or partner. In the final section of the chapter, Topic 2.4 describes the postnatal needs of the family and the range of provision available for the mother and baby.

By the end of this chapter you should be able to recognise and understand:

▶ the biological process of reproduction and problems associated with conception
▶ factors that affect foetal development and a woman's health during pregnancy
▶ the range of checks and tests that are available to monitor the health of the mother and baby
▶ that parents need to prepare for the birth of their child
▶ the stages of labour, methods of delivery and pain relief options
▶ that there are a range of postnatal services available to monitor and promote the health and wellbeing of the mother and baby, and support the family.

Reproduction

 Getting started

This topic focuses on the process of human reproduction and the very beginning of a new life. On completion of this topic you should:

- know about the structure and function of both the male and female reproductive systems
- be able to describe the process of conception for single and multiple babies
- know about the growth and development of the baby in the uterus (womb)
- understand some of the causes of and treatments for infertility.

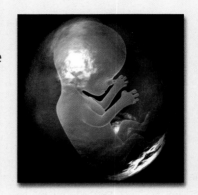

Key terms

Binovular: non-identical twins conceived from two fertilised ova (eggs)

Conception: fertilisation of the female ovum (egg) by the male sperm

Embryo: a fertilised ovum from conception to the eighth week of pregnancy

Implantation: the embedding of the fertilised ovum into the wall of the uterus (womb)

Infertility: the inability to conceive a child

In vitro fertilisation (IVF): an artificial method of conception where fertilisation takes place in a laboratory

Oestrogen: a female hormone produced in the ovary

Ovulation: the release of an ovum from the ovary

Progesterone: a female hormone produced in the ovary

Testosterone: the male sex hormone

Uniovular: identical twins conceived from one fertilised ovum

Human reproduction

A baby is created through the process of **conception**. Both the male and female reproductive systems need to be functioning effectively for conception to take place.

The female reproductive system

The female sex hormones **oestrogen** and **progesterone** are produced by the ovaries and control the female menstrual cycle. An average menstrual cycle lasts 28 days. During the first part of the cycle, the lining of the uterus (womb) thickens. Around day 14 of the cycle, a female ovum (egg) is released from the ovary into the fallopian tube, a process called **ovulation**. If the ovum is not fertilised by a male sperm, then it will be expelled with the lining of the uterus as a menstrual bleed.

The male reproductive system

The testes produce the male sex hormone **testosterone**, which stimulates sperm production. Sperm are made in the testes and stored in the epididymis. When a

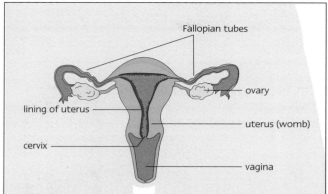

Figure 2.1 The female reproductive system

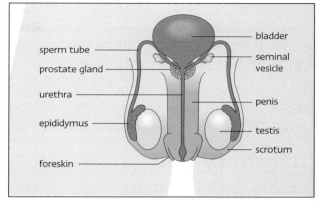

Figure 2.2 The male reproductive system

man becomes aroused, the sperm mixes with seminal fluid from the seminal vesicles to form semen. Semen is ejected from the penis in an ejaculation. During sexual intercourse, sperm are deposited in the vagina and swim up through the female reproductive system to reach the fallopian tubes.

Fertilisation

After ovulation, the ripe ovum travels along the fallopian tube to the uterus. This journey usually takes 5 to 7 days. If sexual intercourse takes place during this time, the egg may become fertilised by a male sperm in the fallopian tube. The fertilised ovum will then attach itself to the wall of the uterus. This is called **implantation**. The fertilised egg will then start to develop into an **embryo**.

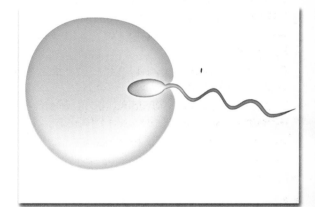

 Over to you!

Can you label the key parts of both the male and female reproductive systems?

Twins

Occasionally, more than one ripe ovum may be released into the fallopian tube at ovulation. This may result in twins or multiple embryos developing.

Identical twins

Identical twins are conceived when the fertilised ovum splits into two and develops into two separate embryos, both sharing the same placenta. Identical twins are also called **uniovular** (one ovum) twins and will always be the same gender (boy/boy or girl/girl).

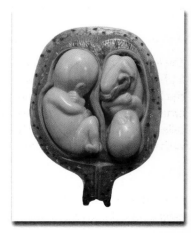

Non-identical twins

Non-identical twins are conceived when two ova are released at the same time and both become fertilised by different sperm. They will develop into two embryos, each with their own placenta. Non-identical twins are also called fraternal or **binovular** (two ova) twins and can be either the same gender or boy/girl.

Over to you!

Discuss with a partner how you might cope with bringing up twins. What challenges do you think you might have to face? What specific challenges might you face if you had identical twins?

Infertility

There are many reasons why conception may not take place. A woman's inability to conceive and a man's inability to impregnate a woman is called **infertility**. It can result from problems with either the male or the female reproductive systems but can also occur for no obvious physical reason. Typical reasons for infertility include, for example:

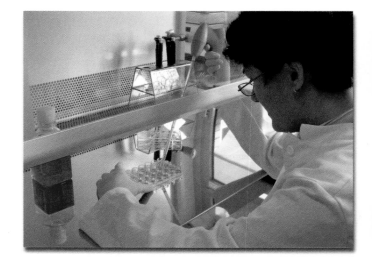

- ▶ hormone imbalance (male or female)
- ▶ blocked fallopian tubes (female)
- ▶ low sperm count (male)
- ▶ damaged, abnormally shaped sperm (male)
- ▶ side-effects of medication (male and female)
- ▶ formation of scar tissue (female)
- ▶ obstruction in sperm-carrying tubes (male)
- ▶ testicular injury or disease (male)
- ▶ erection or ejaculation problems (male).

There are several kinds of infertility treatment, but one of the most commonly used is **in vitro fertilisation (IVF)**. This is a complex medical procedure that involves removing ripened ova (eggs) from the female and fertilising them with male sperm in controlled laboratory conditions. The fertilised ova are then re-implanted into the female uterus and, if the procedure is successful, at least one fertilised ovum will develop into an embryo. This procedure may result in two or more embryos developing, which may lead to the birth of twins or multiple babies.

Activity

The fertility unit at your local hospital has decided to update the information they give to people who use their services. The most common question asked by couples who come for a consultation is: 'Why can't we produce a baby?' The second most popular question is: 'How can you help us to have a baby?' You have been asked to:

• produce an information leaflet that explains the causes of infertility

• describe forms of treatment that are used to help infertile couples conceive.

Use the internet, libraries and other resources to obtain suitable information. You should then use your findings to design and produce a clear, easy-to-follow information leaflet.

Over to you!

Think about what might lead to a couple deciding on infertility treatment. In pairs or small groups, discuss the possible advantages and disadvantages of this decision.

Topic check

1 Describe the female menstrual cycle.
2 How does fertilisation take place?
3 What are the names of the male and female sex hormones?
4 How are uniovular twins conceived?
5 Describe the differences between uniovular and binovular twins.
6 Describe the process of in vitro fertilisation (IVF).

Pregnancy and antenatal provision

Getting started

This topic is about the development of the baby in the uterus (womb) and the different factors that can influence this. It examines the importance of good health in pregnancy and the significance of antenatal care. On completion of this topic you should:

- know about the stages of development of the baby in the uterus and the different stages of pregnancy
- understand the importance of health during pregnancy
- be able to describe routine antenatal checks and specialised tests
- understand the roles of different health professionals involved in antenatal care
- know about parenting classes and recognise the importance of the father/partner.

Key terms

Alpha-fetoprotein (AFP): a specialised blood test in pregnancy that can detect some abnormalities

Antenatal: the period between conception and birth

Amniotic fluid: the liquid that surrounds the foetus in the amniotic sac

Amniotic sac: the sac in which the foetus develops in the uterus

Breech: the position of the baby in the uterus lying bottom or feet first (instead of head first)

Chorionic villus sampling (CVS): a specialised test in pregnancy that removes a sample of the placenta and checks for Down's syndrome

Ectopic pregnancy: an embryo developing outside of the uterus

Embryo: a fertilised ovum from conception to the eighth week of pregnancy

Foetal alcohol syndrome: an abnormality that can affect the developing baby if the mother drinks alcohol during pregnancy

Foetus: the developing baby from the eighth week of pregnancy until birth

Health visitor: a qualified health professional who provides help and support to families with young children

Midwife: a qualified health professional who provides help and support during pregnancy, and during and after birth

Miscarriage: the spontaneous end of a pregnancy and loss of the foetus

Obstetrician: a doctor who specialises in the medical care of women during pregnancy and birth

Placenta: the organ that nourishes the foetus in the uterus

Pre-eclampsia: a condition in pregnancy with high blood pressure, which can be dangerous to the developing foetus

Rubella: the German measles virus

Toxoplasmosis: a disease passed on from contact with cat faeces, which can cause damage to the developing foetus

Trimester: a period in pregnancy, roughly equivalent to 12 weeks

Umbilical cord: connects the foetus with the placenta

Viable: the stage when the foetus is capable of surviving outside of the uterus

Development of the embryo and foetus

The growth and development of the baby in the uterus (womb) is one of the most rapid and exciting periods in child development. It usually takes place over 37 to 42 weeks (full-term pregnancy) and can be divided into three different periods (**trimesters**).

The first trimester

The first 12 weeks of pregnancy are referred to as the first trimester. Once the fertilised ovum has implanted in the wall of the uterus, the **embryo** will begin to grow and develop. This is one of the most critical times in the pregnancy. The growing embryo is nourished directly from the mother's blood through the **placenta**, to which it is attached by the **umbilical cord**. It receives both nutrients and oxygen in this way and therefore does not breathe normally or need to digest food.

The placenta also removes waste products from the embryo and transfers them back into the mother's bloodstream. The embryo is protected in the uterus within the **amniotic sac** and surrounded by **amniotic fluid**. This protective environment keeps the embryo at a constant temperature and helps to prevent some infections. However, some harmful substances like nicotine and certain drugs can cross the placenta and cause damage to the developing embryo (see Health in pregnancy on page 30).

From the eighth week of pregnancy, the embryo is referred to as a **foetus**. Most of the major body organs are formed during this period, although they will take more time to reach full maturity. By 12 weeks, an average foetus measures 6 cm (2.5 in) and weighs 9–14 g (0.5 oz).

Some women experience 'morning sickness' during the first trimester. This is a normal reaction to hormonal changes and it usually improves after the first trimester.

The first trimester is also the most common time for a **miscarriage** to occur, when the embryo is expelled from the uterus, thus terminating the pregnancy. A miscarriage can happen because the fertilised ovum does not implant properly into the wall of the uterus, but can also happen as a result of smoking, drinking alcohol or taking drugs during pregnancy.

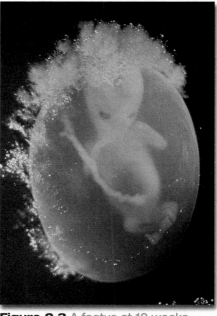

Figure 2.3 A foetus at 12 weeks

Ectopic pregnancy

Occasionally, the fertilised ovum does not implant in the uterus, but in the fallopian tube instead. This is called an **ectopic pregnancy** and the fertilised ovum cannot develop properly. It may result in a miscarriage, or sometimes has to be surgically removed.

Activity

Use the internet, library or other resources to investigate some of the factors that can affect the growth and development of the embryo and foetus in the first trimester of pregnancy. Make a chart that highlights:

1. the factor
2. the possible effects on the embryo
3. how this could be prevented.

The second trimester

Weeks 12 to 25 mark the second trimester of the pregnancy. It is a period of rapid growth for the foetus, and from about week 20 the pregnant woman can usually feel the foetus kicking. By 24 weeks, the foetus is considered to be **viable**, that is able to survive on its own outside of the uterus. At this stage an average foetus measures 21 cm (8 in) and weighs 700 g (1.5 lb). Most women will appear to be noticeably pregnant during this trimester as the uterus increases in size and the breasts also enlarge.

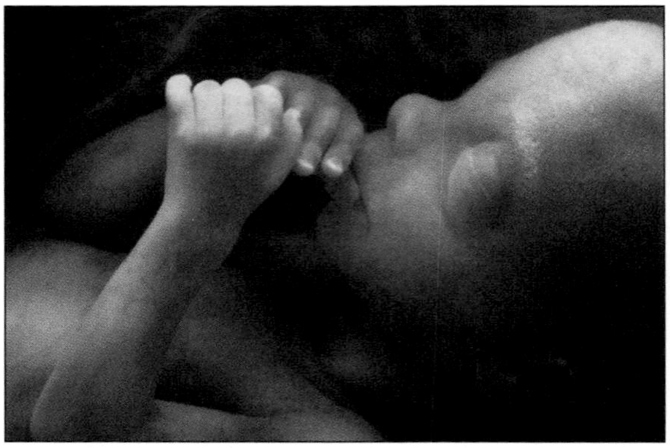

The third trimester

The period from week 25 until full term (between 37 and 42 weeks) marks the third trimester of the pregnancy. The foetus will grow very rapidly during this time in preparation for birth and life outside of the uterus. Towards the end of the third trimester, the baby will settle low in the uterus with the head facing downwards (engaged). Occasionally, the baby will settle with its bottom, legs or feet facing downwards (**breech** position), but in most cases it will turn around before the birth. At full term, an average baby measures 50 cm (20 in) and weighs 3.5 kg (7lb 7oz). Many women experience tiredness and backache at this stage in the pregnancy as the foetus is quite heavy now.

Figure 2.4 A foetus at 25 weeks

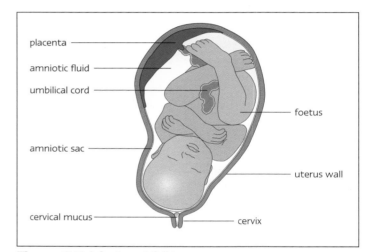

Figure 2.5 A foetus at full term

Activity

Create a 'Pregnancy Timeline' from conception to full term. Include some of the major milestones of growth and development in each trimester.

Health in pregnancy

The health of the mother is extremely important throughout pregnancy, particularly in relation to eating healthily, taking regular exercise and avoiding damaging substances that could potentially harm the developing baby.

Research has shown that smoking in pregnancy can increase the chance of miscarriage, premature birth and low birth weight and this puts the new baby more at risk right from the start. Drinking alcohol during pregnancy can increase the risk of **foetal alcohol syndrome**, which can cause developmental problems for the baby.

Pregnant women should not take any medicines that are not prescribed by a doctor. Some drugs, like heroin and cocaine, can cause the baby to be born addicted.

Infectious diseases like German measles (**rubella**) should also be avoided as this can cause damage to the developing embryo like deafness, blindness and heart defects. **Toxoplasmosis** is a disease that is passed on from contact with cat faeces and it can cause damage to the developing embryo. Pregnant women should therefore avoid contact with cat litter trays.

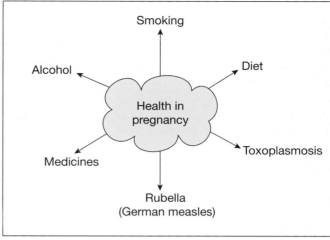

Figure 2.6 Factors affecting health in pregnancy

Healthy eating during pregnancy

The pregnant woman's diet should be well balanced and include all the main nutrients, particularly sources of protein, iron and calcium. The developing foetus will take all the nutrients it requires for its own growth and this can leave the mother's own supply low. She should eat plenty of fresh fruit and vegetables, milk, cheese or other dairy products, and fish, meat, pulses or soya protein.

Some foods contain bacteria that can be harmful to the developing foetus and should therefore be avoided by the pregnant woman. These foods include:

▶ soft cheeses (like brie)

▶ raw eggs (for example in home-made mayonnaise)

▶ undercooked food (particularly frozen foods).

Liver and liver pate should also be avoided as they contain high amounts of Vitamin A that can damage a developing foetus.

 Case study

Aja is a vegetarian and is now 25 weeks pregnant. Her midwife has advised her to eat plenty of protein, iron and calcium in her diet.

1. Investigate some of the foods that contain protein, iron and calcium.
2. Create a nutritionally balanced, full day's menu for Aja (as a vegetarian) showing the sources of these important nutrients.

Antenatal provision

Antenatal provision refers to the care a woman receives during her pregnancy. It includes routine and specialised tests that will be carried out at the antenatal clinic and it also includes the support provided for the couple through parenting classes.

It is important for the pregnant woman to have regular check-ups at the antenatal clinic to make sure that the foetus is growing normally and that there are no complications with the pregnancy. This will include routine tests, like urine and blood pressure, and an abdominal examination by the **midwife** to check on the growth and position of the baby.

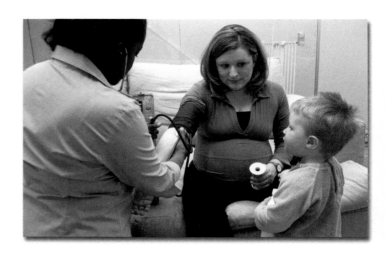

Figure 2.7 Routine checks in pregnancy (carried out at every antenatal clinic visit)

Check	Reason
Mother's weight	• Confirms the baby is growing • Monitors the mother's weight gain
Urine test	• Checks for protein or sugar in the urine (could detect infection or diabetes)
Blood pressure	• High blood pressure is a sign of **pre-eclampsia** (which can be very dangerous for both mother and baby)
Abdominal exam	• Checks the size of the uterus and the foetus • Monitors the growth and position of the foetus

Figure 2.8 Blood tests in pregnancy (carried out at the first antenatal visit)

Test	Reason
Blood group (A B O factor)	Recorded in case the mother needs a blood transfusion at any time (particularly during the birth)
Rhesus factor (positive or negative)	If the mother is Rhesus negative and the baby is Rhesus positive, the mother will need a special injection after the birth to prevent problems with future pregnancies
Rubella	Checks the mother's immunity to rubella (German measles), which can cause damage to the developing embryo
Haemoglobin	Checks the level of iron in the mother's blood (a low iron level could indicate anaemia and the mother may need a supplement)
Hepatitis B	Checks if the mother is a carrier of the Hepatitis B virus, which can harm the developing embryo

Special tests in pregnancy (not carried out routinely at every visit)

Some tests in pregnancy are not carried out routinely at every ante natal visit but may be offered for specific reasons. For example, there may be problems with the mother's health or concerns about the growth and development of the foetus. In some cases there may be a family history of genetic conditions like Down's syndrome. Some of these special tests include the following.

An ultrasound scan

This test uses sound waves to create an image of the foetus in the uterus. The image can be used to monitor the growth of the foetus and to check for certain conditions like spina bifida (an abnormality of the developing spinal cord and nervous system).

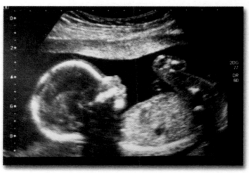

Alpha-fetoprotein blood test (AFP)

This test checks the level of an important protein in the woman's blood. It can be used to detect inherited conditions like Down's syndrome (a genetic abnormality that can result in the child having learning difficulties).

Amniocentesis

This is a very specialised medical test that may be carried out, particularly if there is a family history of certain inherited conditions. A sample of amniotic fluid is withdrawn from the uterus in a carefully monitored procedure using a local anaesthetic. The amniotic fluid is then tested for genetic conditions like Down's syndrome. This test can also determine whether the foetus is male or female.

Chorionic villus sampling (CVS)

This test involves removing a small sample of the placenta while an ultrasound scan is being performed. It can be carried out as early as 10 weeks into the pregnancy and can detect Down's syndrome.

The role of health professionals

Ideally, the first antenatal check-up should take place in the first 12 weeks of pregnancy. This will often be when the woman first suspects that she is pregnant and will visit her general practitioner (GP). Some women may suspect that they are pregnant after missing one or even two periods; they may notice tenderness in and an enlargement of their breasts or may experience some nausea or vomiting. Tiredness, food cravings, more frequent urination, cramping and implantation bleeding or 'spotting' may also occur a little while after ovulation when the fertilised egg attaches itself to the uterine wall and hormone changes begin. The GP may perform an examination to confirm the pregnancy and will be available to provide support throughout the pregnancy if required. Regular checks will then be carried out every month and are usually done by the midwife. A midwife has special training in the care of women before, during and after the birth of the baby. Midwives work in hospitals, clinics and health centres in the community. Some midwives supervise home births and visit new mothers in their own homes.

Activity

Use the internet, library or other resources to investigate inherited conditions like Down's syndrome and spina bifida.

Over to you!

Discuss with a partner some of the challenges you might have to face if you had a baby with Down's syndrome.

From about week 30, antenatal check-ups will become more frequent. Some women may be supported by an **obstetrician** as part of their antenatal care. An obstetrician is a doctor who specialises in pregnancy, labour and birth and will attend the delivery of the baby if there are any complications.

Another health professional who may be involved in antenatal care is the **health visitor**. Health visitors are trained nurses with additional experience in family health and child development. They offer support and advice to all families with children under the age of 5 years.

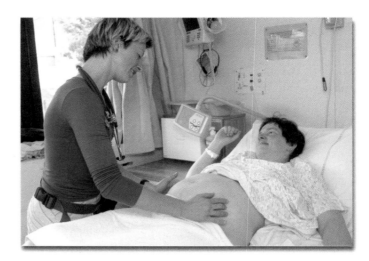

Activity

Talk to someone who has had a baby (this could be someone in your family, a friend or neighbour who is willing to talk to you). Ask about:
- Which health professionals provided support during pregnancy?
- What support was offered?
- What did the person feel about the support offered during pregnancy?
- What advice would the person offer to a newly pregnant mother about support from health professionals?

Parenting classes

During the third trimester of the pregnancy, many couples choose to enrol in parenting classes. These sessions are usually led by the midwife, and topics often include:

▶ preparing for labour and birth (including breathing exercises and pain relief)

▶ the needs of a newborn baby

▶ practical baby care (infant feeding, bathing, nappy changing)

▶ the responsibilities of becoming a parent.

The classes provide a good opportunity for the couple to meet with the midwife and other health professionals and to ask questions, seek out information and receive advice and support.

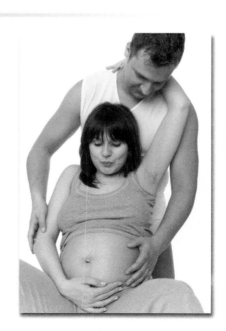

Fathers or partners are always encouraged to attend parenting classes. They can offer support to the pregnant woman, help with relaxation and breathing exercises and learn about what to expect during the process of labour and birth. It is also a good opportunity for fathers or partners to start sharing in the responsibility of becoming a parent and caring for the new baby.

Case study

Aja is now 32 weeks pregnant and she and Ryan have decided to join a parenting class at their local health centre.

In pairs or small groups, discuss and make a list of some of the questions Aja and Ryan may have about the pregnancy, labour and birth process and the responsibilities of becoming new parents.

Topic check

1   What are some of the factors that can affect the growth and development of the baby in the uterus?
2   Describe the routine checks that are carried out at each antenatal visit.
3   Explain two of the more specialised tests that may be carried out during pregnancy.
4   Describe the functions of the:
    - placenta
    - umbilical cord
    - amniotic fluid.
5   Describe the role of the midwife.
6   Explain the importance of attending regular antenatal check-ups.

Preparation for the birth of the new baby

Getting started

This topic is all about the process of birth and the choices available for delivery of the baby. It examines the support available for parents during the birth process and the different methods of delivery. It also considers some of the practical preparations that need to be made for a baby, like buying clothes and nursery equipment. On completion of this topic you should:

- be able to describe the stages of labour and the process of birth
- know about the choices available for the delivery of the baby, including methods of pain relief
- be able to describe the support available for new parents
- know some of the practical preparations that parents may need to make for the new baby.

Key terms

Attachment: the important emotional relationship between a baby and its adult carers (also called 'bonding')

Birth plan: a written outline that identifies a couple's preferences for the birth of their baby

Caesarean section: a surgical procedure that involves cutting open the uterus to deliver the baby

Contractions: tightening of the muscles of the uterus during labour

Crowning: the appearance of the baby's head towards the end of labour

Entonox: a pain-relieving gas that can be breathed by the woman during labour

Epidural anaesthetic: a pain-relieving injection given into the lower back during labour to numb sensation

Episiotomy: a small cut made to widen the opening of the vagina to ease the delivery of the baby

Induce: to start labour artificially

Labour: the three stages of giving birth, beginning with the first contractions of the uterus and ending with the delivery of the baby and the placenta

Obstetrician: a doctor who specialises in the medical care of women during pregnancy and birth

Paediatrician: a doctor who specialises in the medical care of children

Pethidine: a pain-relieving injection given during labour

Premature labour: labour that begins spontaneously before the 37th week of pregnancy

Transcutaneous electrical nerve stimulation (TENS): a device that blocks pain signals during labour

The birth plan

The birth of a baby is usually anticipated with a mixture of excitement and anxiety. As part of routine antenatal care, most couples will develop a **birth plan** with their midwife. This will involve discussing the options available in preparation for the birth of the baby.

Over to you!

Think about some of the choices that couples may need to make as they approach the birth of their baby. What might be some of their major concerns?

Figure 2.9 Planning the birth – issues to discuss

Where the birth will take place
Most babies are born in hospital, but some couples may want to explore the possibility of a home birth. A hospital birth is often recommended for women having their first baby, as there is medical help on hand should any complications arise. A home birth can be a more natural experience, but medical back-up should always be organised in case of emergencies.
Choices for pain relief in labour
Some women may choose a 'natural childbirth' with no pain relief at all. Others may want to have as much pain relief as possible (see page 39).
Will the father/partner be present?
This is a very personal choice, but fathers/partners will always be encouraged to be present, not only to support the mother during labour, but to share in the whole birth experience.

Over to you!

In pairs or groups, discuss the advantages and disadvantages of both a home birth and a hospital birth. Make a chart to summarise your conclusions.

The process of birth

The process of birth is called **labour** and is well named, as the woman's body will be working hard to push the baby out of the uterus.

Labour usually lasts for several hours and can be a worrying time. It is sensible for the process to be monitored by a midwife or other suitably qualified health professional. If there have been complications with the pregnancy, then an **obstetrician** (doctor specialising in pregnancy and birth) may also be present. If problems with the baby are anticipated, then a **paediatrician** (doctor specialising in child health) will also be there.

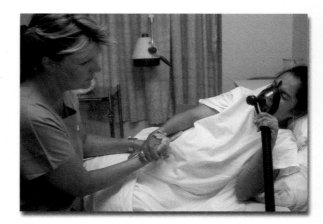

The onset of labour

Labour usually begins with **contractions** (the muscles of the uterus tightening up and getting ready to push the baby out). The amniotic sac may also burst, releasing amniotic fluid. This is often referred to as the 'breaking of the waters' and is a common sign of the onset of labour. The woman may also experience a 'show', which is the release of a blood and mucus discharge from the cervix (neck of the uterus). Contractions will vary in length and intensity, usually starting quite mildly but becoming stronger and closer together as the labour progresses.

Labour is generally divided into three stages.

Stage one

This involves steady contractions of the uterus that open up the cervix wide enough for the baby to pass through (usually about 10 cm). This stage can take several hours, with the contractions becoming more intense.

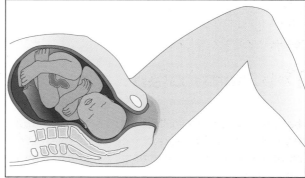

Figure 2.10a Stage 1 of labour

Stage two

Stage two begins when the cervix has fully opened up (fully dilated) and consists of strong, frequent contractions to push the baby out. This is a very active stage of labour and the woman will be pushing with each contraction. She will also be encouraged to use special breathing techniques to help her. A special moment comes when the baby's head finally becomes visible (called **crowning**) and this is usually a sign that the baby will soon be born. The midwife will monitor the process of labour very closely and will record the strength of the contractions and the baby's heart rate.

Once the baby is born, mucus will be cleared from its nose and mouth and it will usually take its first breath. Then the umbilical cord will be clamped and cut, permanently separating the baby from the mother. The new parents will then be able to hold their newborn baby for the first time. This is a very special time and extremely important for the process of **attachment** (bonding), which begins right from the moment of birth. Research has shown that immediate skin-to-skin contact, cuddling the baby closely and making eye contact will all help to strengthen the attachment relationship between parents and their new baby and have real benefits for the child's emotional development in later life.

The new mother may also be encouraged to breastfeed the baby at this time.

Stage three

This consists of expelling the placenta (afterbirth) from the uterus. It is usually a straightforward process guided by the midwife and requires very little effort from the mother. Labour is now complete.

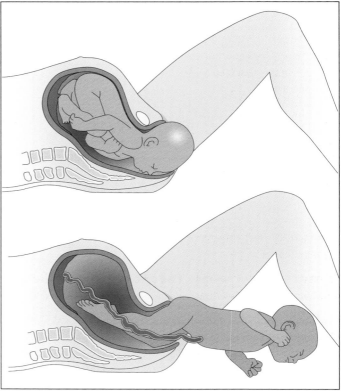

Figure 2.10b Stage 2 of labour

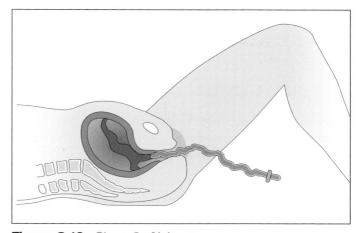

Figure 2.10c Stage 3 of labour

Activity

Use the internet, library or other resources to investigate attachment (bonding) and its importance for the child's emotional development.

Summarise the types of behaviour that can encourage a strong attachment between parents and their babies.

Pain relief in labour

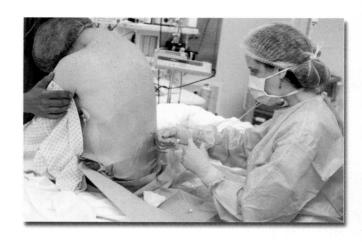

There are several methods of pain relief that a woman may choose to use during labour. These will be discussed with the midwife and should be outlined on the birth plan.

A pain relieving injection such as **pethidine** may be given during the first stage of labour. This helps to relieve the pain of strong contractions, but it can affect the baby's breathing, so would only be given in the early stages of labour.

A mixture of nitrous oxide and oxygen (**Entonox**), often called 'gas and air', can be breathed through a mask to relieve the pain of contractions. This has no harmful effects on the baby and can therefore be used during all stages of labour.

Some women may choose to have an **epidural anaesthetic**. This is carefully injected into the woman's lower back and it numbs sensation from the waist downwards.

An alternative form of pain relief is **transcutaneous electrical nerve stimulation (TENS)**, which works by blocking pain signals using a gentle electrical current passed through pads attached to the mother's back. There are a number of alternative methods of pain relief available in some hospitals, including aromatherapy, reflexology, hypnosis and acupuncture.

Activity

Make a chart that shows the advantages and disadvantages of different types of pain relief in labour. In pairs or small groups, discuss some of the factors that may need to be considered when making a choice about which method to use.

Complications during labour

Sometimes, labour and delivery of the baby do not always progress normally. Problems can occur that require different approaches in order for the baby to be born safely.

Induction of labour

Sometimes labour does not begin spontaneously at full term. If pregnancy continues beyond 42 weeks, it can become more dangerous for the baby to stay in the uterus. It may then be decided to **induce** labour (start it artificially) by giving the woman a drug that will begin the process of birth.

Sometimes, labour may be induced before full term. This might be due to complications in pregnancy, like high blood pressure, which can be dangerous for the baby.

Premature labour

Sometimes labour may start spontaneously before full term. When this happens before 37 weeks, it is called **premature labour**. The more premature the labour is, the more dangerous it will be for the baby. However, with modern technology and special intensive care units, babies have been known to survive when born at 23 or even 22 weeks and weighing only 500 g.

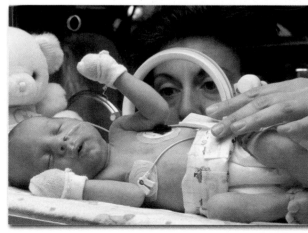

Forceps delivery

Forceps may be used to help the delivery of the baby if the mother has been pushing for a long time and the baby is not making progress. An **episiotomy** (a small cut to widen the opening of the vagina) will usually be made to ease the delivery and this will be stitched up after the birth.

Caesarean section

A **Caesarean section** is a surgical procedure that involves cutting open the uterus in order for the baby to be born. It is performed under a general anaesthetic or by using an epidural anaesthetic (see Pain relief in labour on page 39). Caesarean sections are often carried out as emergency procedures when the baby has become 'distressed' during a long or difficult labour. Caesarean sections can also be planned in advance. This might happen if the woman has had problems during pregnancy or for the birth of twins.

The role of the father/partner

The role of the father/partner during labour and birth is a very important one. The birth of a baby can be a magical time to share together, and the father/partner can offer comfort and moral support to the mother as well as sharing in the attachment process at this early stage. The father/partner will also have an important role in practical preparations for the new baby. The new parents may want to prepare a nursery, shop for clothing and equipment or arrange to have time off work. Caring for a new baby involves lots of lifestyle adjustments and it is important that the new parents consider this as a shared responsibility right from the start.

Activity

Use the internet, library or other resources to investigate some of the risks involved with:

- premature labour
- Caesarean section delivery.

Case study

Aja and Ryan are approaching the time for the birth of their baby.

In pairs or small groups, discuss and make a list of the different ways that Ryan could support Aja in preparing for the arrival of their new baby and throughout the birth process.

Preparing for the baby

New babies need clothing and nursery equipment and most couples will enjoy focusing on these practical preparations as they wait for the baby's arrival. The first set of clothing for a new baby is often referred to as the layette and will usually consist of vests, all-in-one stretch suits, a hat, socks or bootees and some outer clothing like a pram suit. Clothing for a new baby should be comfortable, warm and washable and parents should not be tempted to buy too many items, as babies soon outgrow the newborn sizes.

All babies need nappies and parents will need to decide whether to use terry towelling or reusable nappies (which need to be washed), or disposable ones (which are thrown away).

Over to you!

Think about the factors involved with different kinds of nappies. Which type would you use?

Essential nursery equipment usually includes a pram, pushchair or buggy, and a cot or carrycot of some kind. Many items of nursery equipment can be bought second hand, although it is important to make sure that all equipment is safe and has a British Standard Kitemark safety label. Cots should be sturdy, with a well-fitting mattress and bars that are no more than 6 cm apart. Prams need to be well balanced and weather resistant, with secure brakes. Parents need to consider their lifestyle and home environment when thinking about the equipment to buy for their baby. A family who travels mostly by car will need a car seat for the baby, whereas a light, collapsible buggy might be better for travelling on the bus. Some items of nursery equipment are non-essential and parents will need to consider their budget carefully.

 Activity

Investigate the advantages and disadvantages of different types of prams and pushchairs. Consider factors like cost, safety and lifestyle, and make a chart using ICT to illustrate your findings.

 Case study

Aja and Ryan are making preparations for their baby. They do not own a car and they live in a one-bedroom flat with no garden, but close to a large park. They do not have a lot of spare money, but would like to purchase some essential clothing and nursery equipment ready for the baby's arrival.

Investigate and select items of clothing and essential nursery equipment for Aja and Ryan's baby, listing the cost and reasons for purchase of each item.

The most important part of preparing for a new baby is to make sure that it will be welcomed into a loving home. Babies respond right from birth to the sights and sounds around them. They need to be cuddled, talked to and smiled at by caring adults who keep them safe, warm and secure.

 Topic check

1 What are some of the issues that might be discussed as part of the birth plan?
2 Describe briefly the three stages of labour.
3 What do you understand by the term 'attachment'?
4 Describe the roles of the:
   • midwife   • obstetrician   • paediatrician.
5 Explain the different kinds of pain relief that may be used during labour.
6 List three important factors to consider when buying the following equipment for a new baby:
   • pushchair   • cot.

Postnatal care

▶ Getting started

This topic is all about the care and support available for the baby and the new family in the first few weeks after the birth. It covers the mother's health after the birth of the baby, including the importance of good nutrition. It also explores the needs of a new family and the support available from different professionals. On completing this topic you should:

- know about the support available for families with a new baby
- understand the importance of postnatal check-ups for both mother and baby
- know about the importance of good nutrition in the postnatal period.

🔑 Key terms

Attachment: the important emotional relationship between a baby and its adult carers (also called 'bonding')

Family support worker: provides help and guidance with parenting skills and advice about other support services for families

Health visitor: a qualified health professional who provides help and support to families with young children

Lactation: the production of breast milk for breastfeeding

Midwife: a qualified health professional who provides help and support in pregnancy, and during and after birth

Postnatal depression: a serious form of depression that can affect some women after the birth of the baby

Postnatal period: the first 6 weeks after the birth of the baby

Postnatal care

Following the birth of a baby, the mother's body needs to recover physically and adjust emotionally. This process starts during the **postnatal period**, which usually refers to the first 6 weeks after the birth. During this time, the mother's uterus (womb) will be returning to its normal size, her body will be returning to its pre-pregnant state and her breasts will start to produce milk (the process of **lactation**).

The mother's emotions will be influenced by hormone levels, which are returning to normal after the birth. These hormones can affect the mother's moods and behaviour during the postnatal period. Taking care of a newborn baby is a big responsibility and the new family will also start adjusting to this during the postnatal period. Postnatal care refers to the help and support offered to the baby, the mother and the new family unit as they start to make these adjustments.

Help and support

The **midwife** will provide support during the first 10 days after the birth and will check on the health and wellbeing of both the mother and the baby. The midwife will examine the mother to make sure that her body is recovering physically. It is important that the mother eats a nutritious, balanced diet, gets plenty of rest and sleep and starts to gain confidence in caring for the new baby. The process of **attachment** (bonding) is extremely important in this postnatal period and the midwife will support the new parents in developing a close relationship with their baby. This can be encouraged through lots of cuddling, talking to the baby and making sure that the parents attend to all the baby's basic needs. The midwife will also provide support with breastfeeding if necessary, helping the mother establish a feeding routine that satisfies the baby's needs. The production of breast milk (lactation) relies on the mother having a good, balanced diet with all the essential nutrients, but particularly protein, calcium and iron. The midwife will also examine the baby, carry out routine checks and make sure the baby is gaining weight.

The **health visitor** is another professional who will provide support for the new family. As a qualified nurse, with additional training in family health and child development, the health visitor will support the parents with practical aspects of baby care, including bathing, nappy changing, feeding and sleeping routines. The new mother can also visit the health visitor at baby clinics, which are usually held at the health centre or local children's centre. Baby clinics provide a supportive environment where new mothers can check on their baby's progress and weight, as well as gain information and advice about child development, health checks and routine immunisations.

A **family support worker** may work with some new families to help them adjust to the demands of parenting and encourage them to access other services that provide support, for example local groups where parents and their children can meet each other, share ideas and discuss their worries and concerns.

 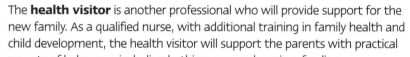 **Case study**

Kerry gave birth to Alicia 5 weeks ago in the local hospital. Her labour was uncomplicated and the birth process was normal. Kerry's partner Melvin was with her the whole time and they were able to enjoy the arrival of their daughter together. Alicia weighed 3.2 kg at birth. Kerry spent one night in the hospital and has been at home with Alicia since then. The midwife has visited regularly and is satisfied that Alicia is breastfeeding well and gaining weight. Kerry seems to be adjusting well and responding positively to her new role as a mother. The health visitor has arranged to see Kerry with Alicia at the baby clinic next week for a routine check-up.

1. What are some of the questions Kerry might have for the health visitor?

2. What are some of the questions the health visitor might have for Kerry?

3. What foods (and essential nutrients) should Kerry be eating to maintain lactation while she is breastfeeding?

Over to you!

In pairs or small groups, discuss the kind of support you might need as a new parent, particularly if you had no family living locally or if you were new to the area.

Activity

Find out where your local health centre or children's centre is located. Investigate the services available there for new families in the area.

Postnatal depression

A common problem for new mothers during the postnatal period is 'baby blues'. This is a condition caused by changing hormone levels that affect the woman's moods and can make her very easily upset. This condition is usually short lived and, with support from a sensitive partner and advice from health professionals, most women will cope with this. However, this can develop into a more serious condition called **postnatal depression**, which can have more long-term effects on the mother's emotional state and mental health. This should always be carefully monitored as the woman may need specialist psychiatric help.

Activity

Use the internet, library or other resources to investigate postnatal depression and some of the treatments available for women.

In small groups, design a short TV public information broadcast to raise awareness of postnatal depression.

Registering the birth

The parents have a legal duty to register the birth of the baby within 6 weeks (3 weeks in Scotland). This should be done at the registrar's office and a birth certificate will be issued.

The role of the father/partner

The postnatal period can be a difficult time for the father/partner as much of the attention will be focused on the baby and the new mother. It is very easy for fathers to feel 'left out' and yet it is an important time for them to be involved, as they adjust to the demands of being a new parent and start to form an attachment with the baby.

Topic check

1 Explain what is involved in postnatal care.
2 Describe the role of the health visitor.
3 Give examples of some of the services available at a baby clinic.
4 What do you understand by the term postnatal depression?
5 What nutrients are important for a mother who is breastfeeding?
6 Give examples of some of the foods that contain these nutrients.

3 Physical growth and development

Introduction

This chapter is divided into four topics:

3.1 The new baby

3.2 Physical development norms

3.3 Conditions for physical development

3.4 Child safety

This chapter describes the early stages of physical growth and development, from birth to 5 years of age. Topic 3.1 describes the characteristics and needs of newborn babies, including the special care required for premature and low birth weight babies. Topic 3.2 outlines the stages and 'norms' of physical growth and development, describing the physical changes that occur between birth and 5 years of age. Topic 3.3 focuses on the conditions, clothing and footwear a child needs to promote and support their physical growth and development between birth and 5 years of age. In the final section of this chapter, Topic 3.4 describes the safety needs of young children and the ways in which they can be safeguarded inside and outside of the home.

By the end of this chapter you should be able to recognise and understand:

▶ the characteristics and care needs of newborn babies

▶ the special care needs of premature babies

▶ the physical growth and development norms of children under 5

▶ the importance of providing appropriate conditions, clothing and footwear to promote and support the physical growth and development of babies and young children

▶ that babies and young children face a range of safety hazards and risks at home and in outdoor environments.

The new baby

 Getting started

This section is about the newborn baby. It covers the appearance and basic needs of all babies and the special needs of premature babies. When you have completed this topic you should:

- know about the appearance and abilities of a newborn baby
- understand the baby's need for love, food, warmth, sleep and protection
- be able to describe the special care of premature and low birth weight babies
- know about reducing the risk of cot death.

 Key terms

Birthmark: a blemish on the skin that is formed before birth

Cot death: the sudden and unexplained death of a baby, usually while sleeping

Fontanelle: the soft spot on top of a baby's head

Hypothermia: a dangerous condition that occurs when the body temperature falls below 35.5°C

Incubator: a specialised piece of equipment used to support premature or low birth weight babies

Jaundice: a yellowness of the skin and eyes due to the immaturity of a newborn baby's liver

Neonate: the name given to a baby in the first 4 weeks of life

Premature: born before 37 weeks of pregnancy

Special care baby unit: a unit in a hospital that provides special care for premature, low birth weight and sick babies

Umbilicus: the navel where the umbilical cord is attached

Vernix: a white greasy substance that protects the baby's skin in the uterus

The newborn baby

A new baby is totally dependent on adult care, which makes being a new parent a very demanding and responsible job. In the first 4 weeks of life, the new baby is referred to as a **neonate**.

Appearance

The appearance of newborn babies can vary quite a lot, but at full term the average measurements are usually:

Weight: 3–3.5 kg (7–7.5 lb)

Length: 50–55 cm (20–22 inches)

Head circumference: 35 cm (13.5 inches)

Routine examination of the newborn baby

Very soon after birth, the newborn baby is examined by a doctor to check for any abnormalities.

Figure 3.1 Routine examinations for newborn babies

Examination	Reason
Eyes	Any infection or visual problems
Mouth	Checking for a cleft palate (roof of the mouth not properly formed)
Heart	Any abnormal heart sounds (heart murmur)
Fingers and toes	Checking the correct number of each
Hips	Checking for any dislocation of the hips (treatment may be necessary)
Reflexes Reflex action: i) Sucking and swallowing ii) Rooting iii) Grasp iv) Startle v) Walking vi) Falling (Moro)	Automatic nervous responses that indicate the baby's nervous system is functioning i)A baby will suck on anything placed in the mouth. ii) If the cheek is stroked, the baby will turn the head in that direction, as if searching for the mother's nipple. iii) A baby will grasp tightly onto an object placed in the hand. iv) A baby will clench the hands and move the arms outwards if startled by a loud noise or bright light. v) If held upright with the feet touching a flat surface, the baby will make walking movements. vi) Any sudden movements that affect the neck make the baby feel like it will be dropped. This makes the baby fling out the arms and open the hands.

Around the sixth day after birth, the baby's blood is tested to check for some conditions that could affect future health and development. These include:

▶ Phenylketonuria (PKU) – a very rare condition that affects the baby's ability to digest milk. If it is not treated it can lead to the baby having learning difficulties.

▶ Hypothyroidism – another rare condition that affects the baby's growth and development. It can also lead to learning difficulties if not treated.

▶ Cystic fibrosis – a condition that causes long-term lung disease. Early treatment can improve the child's health, although there is no complete cure.

Skin

At birth, the baby's skin is still usually covered with **vernix** but this is absorbed into the skin within a few days. Some babies are born with **birthmarks** on their skin. Most of these will disappear in time, although some may stay for life. Some babies develop a condition called **jaundice** in the first few days after birth that causes their skin to appear yellow. In most cases this clears up without any treatment, but sometimes it can be more serious and the baby may need more specialised care.

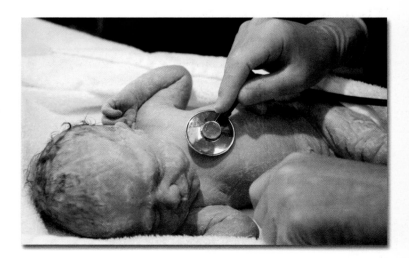

Head

At birth, the baby's head appears much bigger than the rest of the body and this can seem out of proportion. The bones of the skull are still very soft and not completely joined together. This can be felt on top of the baby's head at the **fontanelle** ('soft spot'), which may take about 12–18 months to fully close. Some babies are born with lots of hair and some are completely bald! Babies can see from birth, although their distance vision will develop more fully over time. New babies can also hear from birth and are particularly responsive to the voices of their parents.

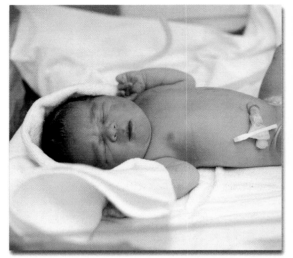

 Over to you!

Think about caring for a newborn baby who is completely dependent on you for all of its basic needs. In pairs or small groups, discuss the impact this would have on your life and the changes you would need to make. How would you cope?

Body

At birth, the umbilical cord is clamped and cut. There are no nerves in the cord, so this does not hurt the baby at all. The clamp will usually remain in place for a few days as the stump of the cord dries up, to leave a neat **umbilicus** (navel).

The needs of a newborn baby

All newborn babies need:

- to feel loved and cared for
- to feel safe and secure
- food and nourishment
- rest and sleep
- warmth and comfort
- protection from infection, danger and harm.

Love and security

All babies need to feel loved and cared for. They need to be cuddled, rocked, smiled at and talked to. This helps them to feel safe and secure and is a very important part of attachment (bonding). The basic care routines of bathing, nappy changing, feeding and sleeping provide lots of opportunities for close interaction between the parents and their new baby. Babies cry for many different reasons. Crying is their only way of communicating and it could mean they are hungry, thirsty, uncomfortable or in pain. It is very important to pay attention to a crying baby and to provide reassurance and comfort. Babies should never be left to cry for long periods of time.

Food

Milk is the main form of nourishment for all babies in the first 6 months of life. This may be breast milk or specially prepared formula milk given in a bottle. Feeding time is important not only for providing food, but also for the physical closeness between the baby and parent. As the baby gets older, meal times will also become an important social occasion.

Sleep

New babies spend much of their time sleeping, often between 18 and 20 hours a day, although all babies are different in their sleeping patterns. It is important to establish a routine for sleeping, with a regular bedtime as the baby gets older. This helps the baby feel secure and will help the new parents to settle into a care pattern. The sleeping position is very important for new babies, as this has been shown to be a factor in **cot death** (sudden infant death syndrome). Babies should always be put to sleep on their backs ('back to sleep') and with their feet at the bottom of the cot or crib ('feet to foot').

Cot death (sudden infant death syndrome)

The Foundation for the Study of Infant Death recommends the following advice to reduce the risk of cot death:

▶ Always place babies to sleep on their backs and with their feet at the bottom of the cot.

▶ Don't smoke either during pregnancy or in the same room as the baby.

▶ Don't let the baby become too hot – use layers of light bedding and keep the baby's room temperature between 16° C and 20° C.

▶ Don't use a pillow in the baby's cot until they are at least 2 years old.

Warmth

It is very important to keep newborn babies in a consistent, warm environment. New babies cannot control their own body temperature and are very sensitive to changes in room temperature. **Hypothermia** (very low body temperature) can happen quickly in new babies and can be very dangerous. Babies can also become overheated easily if they have too many clothes or blankets on.

Protection

New babies are very vulnerable and rely on adult protection to be safe. They need protecting from hazards both inside and outside the home, and protection from diseases and infections. Parents need to be aware of home safety and hygiene, how to keep babies safe when travelling and the importance of immunisations to protect babies from infectious diseases.

 Activity

Design an information leaflet for parents, outlining how to reduce the risk of cot death.

Case study

Kerry and Melvin's daughter Alicia is now 8 weeks old. She is fully breastfed, is gaining weight normally and seems very content. After her bath, she usually goes to bed around 7pm and sleeps until about 2am, when she wakes for a breastfeed, before going back to sleep until about 6am. Kerry and Melvin live quite near a park and Kerry likes to take Alicia there on most days if it is fine. Kerry has also joined a local group for parents and new babies, which she attends with Alicia on three mornings every week.

Plan a daily routine for Alicia, which meets all her basic needs. Include feeding times, nappy changing, sleep times, bath time and play times. Use ICT to record your plan and include each day from Monday to Friday.

Premature babies

A **premature** baby is born before 37 weeks of pregnancy and will usually have a low birth weight (less than 2.5 kg or 5.5 lbs). Some babies can have a low birth weight even though they are born at full term. This is very common if the mother has smoked during pregnancy. Premature and low birth weight babies need special care because they may have problems with breathing, feeding or maintaining their own body temperature. Specialised care can be given to premature and low birth weight babies in **special care baby units** in the hospital. This special care may involve the baby being in an **incubator**, which keeps the baby at a constant temperature and can monitor the baby's breathing. It can be a frightening experience for parents if their baby needs special care, particularly if it involves complicated machinery. They may need a lot of encouragement to handle and care for their baby so they can still feel close and develop an attachment.

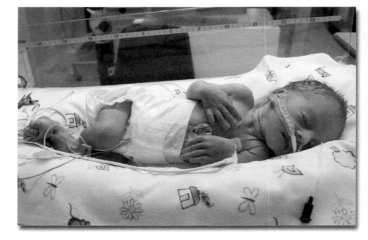

The length of time a baby spends in the special care unit will depend on how premature the baby is and how closely the baby needs to be monitored. Having a new baby on a special care unit can be very demanding for new parents. They will want to spend as much time as possible with the new baby and this can be extremely tiring. It may also cause problems if there are other children in the family who might feel left out because mum and dad are spending so much time at the hospital.

Medical technology and the dedicated staff in special care units help to support the survival of even the tiniest babies.

Activity

Use the internet, library or other resources to investigate the smallest babies to be born alive and survive. What kinds of problems do these babies face?

Over to you!

In pairs or small groups, discuss some of the challenges you might face in caring for a baby so small.

Topic check

1 Describe the appearance of a newborn baby.
2 Explain some of the routine checks carried out on all newborn babies.
3 What are the basic needs of all babies?
4 Explain how you would meet a baby's need for protection.
5 What are the special needs of premature babies?
6 What are some of the ways to reduce the risk of cot death?

Physical development norms

▶ Getting started

This topic is all about the normal physical development of a baby and child from birth to 5 years old. It looks at how a child's progress is monitored and some of the factors that can affect development. It focuses on the main stages of physical development and different ways to encourage this. On completion of this topic you should:

■ know about the normal stages of physical development

■ understand some of the factors that can influence development

■ be able to describe some of the ways to encourage children's physical development at different stages.

Key terms

Developmental screening tests: regular check-ups to monitor a child's development

Fine motor skills: the use of hand and finger movements

Gross motor skills: the use of large body movements

Hand–eye coordination: the ability to make the hands work together with what the eyes can see

Manipulative task: precise, detailed task that requires the use of small hand and finger movements

Milestones: norms used for monitoring a child's development

Palmar grasp: using the whole of the hand to pick up and hold objects

Pincer grasp: using the thumb and index finger to pick up and hold small objects

Prone position: lying on the stomach

Tripod grasp: using the thumb and first two fingers to hold objects

Stages of development

It is very important to remember that every child is different. Child development is a process and every child will progress in their own individual way. Some children will begin to walk at a very early age and be later learning to talk; other children will be early talkers and take more time learning to walk. All areas of development are linked and it is important to view the child as a whole person.

A child's development is monitored using **milestones**, or development norms. Milestones provide an average guide for assessing a child's progress, but it is important to remember that there is a very wide range of normal and every child will progress at a different rate. A child's development will be monitored using **developmental screening tests**, which are carried out at specific stages and are usually assessed by the health visitor. These tests provide a general guide only, but are a useful record that the child is progressing normally.

Physical

- Learning to move and coordinate the body.

Intellectual

- Learning to think and understand information.
- Learning to communicate.

CHILD DEVELOPMENT

Emotional

- Learning to be confident and independent.

Social

- Learning to get along with others.

Figure 3.2 The main areas of child development

Influences on development

There are many different factors that can influence a child's development at different stages, including:

▶ during pregnancy, if, for example, the woman becomes infected with rubella (German measles)

▶ at birth, if, for example, the baby is born prematurely

▶ genetic conditions the child may have inherited, such as Down's syndrome

▶ encouragement and care, for example how the child is stimulated and the environment in which the child is brought up.

> **Activity**
>
> Use the internet, library or other resources to investigate Down's syndrome and the different ways it can influence a child's development.

Physical development

Physical development is the development of the child's body and physical skills. It relies on the development of muscles, which are stimulated by the baby's developing brain. Physical development starts from the top, and all babies will learn to control their neck muscles (head control) before their back muscles (sitting up) and finally their leg muscles (standing and walking).

The main areas of physical development are:

▶ **gross motor skills** – the development of large movements, balance and body coordination (like running, skipping and kicking a ball)

▶ **fine motor skills** – the development of hand movements (like grasping, fastening buttons and using scissors)

▶ body functioning – the development of physical and sensory abilities (like vision, hearing, and bladder and bowel control).

Gross motor skills

The development of gross motor skills begins with head control. This involves the baby gaining control of their neck muscles in order to support their head. Newborn babies have very weak neck muscles and their heads should always be well supported.

By the age of 3 months, most babies have developed head control and can lift their head up if they are lying on their stomach (**prone position**). They will start to use their leg muscles by kicking, especially when lying on their back or when supported in the bath.

The muscles of the upper body are the next to develop and this involves the baby gaining control of their arms, hands and back muscles. By the age of 6 months, most babies can sit up with some support and can roll over. They will also start to use their arms to reach out for toys and other objects and are beginning to bear weight on their legs when held securely by an adult.

Over to you!

What is your earliest memory of playing outdoors?

In pairs or small groups, share your ideas about outdoor play and make a list of activities that would encourage young children to enjoy the outdoors.

Not all babies crawl, but most babies find their own way of moving around, such as rolling over and over or shuffling on their bottom. By the age of 9 months, most babies will have developed some way of getting around!

The development of standing and walking requires muscle strength, balance and coordination. Babies need lots of opportunities to practise these skills as their confidence develops and they are finally ready to walk by themselves. By the age of 18 months, most babies will walk sturdily alone, but some will still need to hold on to an adult's hand for extra support.

Case study

Kerry and Melvin's daughter Alicia is now 1 year old. She can pull herself up to a standing position and can walk holding on to the furniture. She can sit by herself for long periods of time without any support and enjoys sitting on the floor to play with her toys. Kerry often takes Alicia to the park in her pushchair and pushes her in a baby swing.

1. How could Kerry encourage Alicia's gross motor skills?

2. What kinds of toys or activities might help?

As the child's movements become more coordinated, they will start to be more adventurous and will experiment with climbing and getting up and down stairs, (although some will have attempted this much earlier). By the age of 2 years, most children will be able to climb confidently onto furniture and walk up and down stairs, using both feet on each step. Playing outside will give toddlers lots of opportunities to practise these new skills and they will enjoy 'sit and ride' toys, running around and learning how to kick a ball.

Activity

Investigate a range of different toys and activities to encourage gross motor skills at different ages. Give examples of two different toys or activities that could encourage gross motor skills with:

- a 6 month old
- a 2½ year old.

Explain how each toy or activity would encourage gross motor skills at each age.

As their gross motor skills continue to develop, children gain more control over their movements. By the age of 3 years, most children can pedal a tricycle and jump with both feet together. Their body coordination will be improving rapidly and they will enjoy trying to catch a large ball, walking on tiptoe and running around obstacles.

Children need lots of stimulation and opportunities to practise their gross motor skills in a safe environment. Lots of praise and encouragement will help children to gain confidence and enjoy developing their physical abilities. They need space to move around and adult support to help them improve their skills.

By the age of 4 years, most children can walk up and down stairs like an adult, pedal and control a tricycle with confidence, and throw, catch and kick a ball with some accuracy. These abilities become more advanced and skilful as the child reaches 5 years old, when most children can skip, hop and play bat and ball games with good coordination.

Fine motor skills

Learning to use their hands and fingers is quite a complicated task for babies and young children. It involves skills like:

▶ grasping – learning to hold objects securely and precisely (like a rattle, a pencil or a spoon)

▶ **hand-eye coordination** – learning to make their hands work together with what their eyes can see (like fitting a piece into a jigsaw puzzle or building a tower of blocks)

▶ manipulation – learning to use their hands and fingers to handle objects precisely (like screwing/unscrewing and threading beads).

Most babies start to play with their hands from about 3 months old. They will spend time just gazing at their hands or may hold a rattle for a short time. Bright, stimulating toys, hung where a baby can see them (such as a mobile or baby gym) will encourage the baby to reach out and grasp, and help to develop hand-eye coordination.

By the age of 6 months, most babies will reach out and grasp an object or toy. They will do this using their whole hand (**palmar grasp**) and will start to pass toys from one hand to the other. As their fine motor skills develop, babies learn to use their fingers more precisely. By the age of 9 months, most babies can use their thumb and index finger to pick up small objects using a **pincer grasp**.

Babies need lots of opportunities to handle objects and develop their fine motor skills. Simple household objects like wooden spoons, small boxes or baskets make ideal toys and encourage babies to use their hands in different ways.

At this age, babies tend to explore everything with their mouth, which means it is very important that any objects given to a baby are completely safe (see Topic 3.4).

By the age of 1 year, most babies can point with their index finger and clap their hands together. Fine motor skills will continue to develop through simple play activities and routine self-help skills like feeding and dressing themselves. By the age of 18 months, most babies can scribble with a crayon and feed themselves with a spoon (which requires a great deal of hand-eye coordination and may be very messy to begin with!).

Most 2 year olds can build a tower of five or six blocks and turn the pages in a book one at a time (a difficult **manipulative task**).

Palmar grasp

Pincer grasp

> **Over to you!**
>
> Think about some of the manipulative activities you enjoyed as a child, (like crayoning, jigsaws or construction toys). What were some of your favourites? Why did you enjoy them?
>
> Share your memories with others in the group.

By the age of 3 years, most children will be starting to use a dominant hand (either right- or left-handed) and can hold a crayon using a **tripod grasp**. They can also thread large beads onto a string and feed themselves using a fork and spoon.

 Activity

Imagine that you are organising a pre-school group for 3 year olds. Investigate a range of toys and activities that encourage fine motor skills at this age, and make a list of some that you would provide for the children in the group.

As muscle strength increases in the hands and fingers, children can use their fine motor skills for more complex tasks. By the age of 4 years, most children can use a pencil to draw a figure with a head, legs and a body, complete a large piece jigsaw puzzle and can cut with safety scissors. At 5 years old, these skills have improved even further and most children can feed themselves with a knife and fork, fasten and unfasten buttons and colour in pictures, staying within the lines.

Body functioning

An important part of physical development includes the development of physical and sensory abilities like vision, hearing, and bladder and bowel control. These skills all develop as the baby's nervous system matures over the first few years of life.

Vision

A baby can see from birth but only at short distances. Newborn babies often appear to have a squint, with one eye focusing in a different direction from the other. This is because the muscles that hold the eyes in a straightforward position are still under-developed and it takes about 6 months for the eyes to work together. By 1 year old, a baby's distant vision is more developed and by 3 years old their vision is fully mature. Vision is checked regularly and all children have an eyesight test on starting school so that any problems can be treated or corrected without delay.

Hearing

Research tells us that babies can hear while still in the uterus, responding to loud noises and the mother's voice. The newborn hearing test will check the baby's hearing at birth and this will continue to be monitored regularly. Being able to hear is an important part of language development, so it is very important that any hearing problems are detected early so treatment can be provided. At 6 months old, most babies will turn towards a sound and by a year old the baby will respond to a wide range of different sounds and familiar voices.

Bladder and bowel control

Control of the bladder and bowels relies on the maturing nervous system and the child gaining control of their muscles. All children will do this at different times and it cannot be rushed. A positive attitude towards toilet training will help the child gain confidence and help them gain independence. Most children will start to indicate their toilet needs between 18 months and 2 years old. By 3 years old many children are dry during the day although it can take longer to gain control throughout the night.

Most children will be independent with their toileting by the age of 5 years.

Activity

Investigate some of the ways that parents can encourage their children with toilet training. Design a leaflet or web page with 'Hints and Tips' for parents to manage this important stage in their child's development.

Teeth

Teeth start growing in the gums while the foetus is developing in the uterus but do not usually start to erupt until the baby is about 6 months old (although some babies are born with teeth!). The first set of teeth are called milk teeth. There are 20 milk teeth in total and they usually appear in a certain order with the lower, central teeth coming first. Babies can be quite fretful when they are teething as their gums will be sore. They often have red cheeks, dribble a lot and chew on their fists and other objects.

After the age of 5 years, the milk teeth will start to fall out and be replaced by the permanent teeth. It is important that children are encouraged to take care of their teeth from a very young age. This helps to develop good dental hygiene habits and can reduce tooth decay. Calcium helps to build strong teeth and children should have plenty of milk, cheese and yogurt in their diet. Sweet foods and drinks should be avoided as they encourage tooth decay. Toddlers should be taught to brush their own teeth after meals and at bedtime with their own brush. Visiting the dentist can begin from a very early age, often when the child goes along with their parent. Dental check-ups should be carried out every 6 months and this helps to establish a lifelong habit.

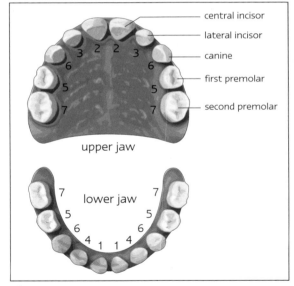

Figure 3.3 Milk teeth

Activity

Design and make a poster to encourage young children to take care of their teeth.

Figure 3.4 Summary of physical development (birth to 5 years)

Age	Gross motor skills	Fine motor skills	Body functioning	Encouragement
Birth	• Walking reflex • No head control	• Grasp reflex • Fists clenched	• Startled by loud noises • Focuses at short distances	• Support the head • Talking, cuddling • Colourful mobiles
3 months	• Some head control • Kicks legs strongly	• Plays with hands • Holds an object for a short time	• Responds to sounds • Follows objects with eyes	• Play on the floor and in the bath • Singing and finger rhymes
6 months	• Sits with some support • Rolls over	• Grasps objects using the palmar grasp • Puts objects in mouth	• Eyes focus together (no squint) • Turns towards sounds • Teething may start	• Clapping games • Peek-a-boo • Rattles to hold • Picture books
9 months	• Pulls up to standing • Sits without support • May start to crawl	• Uses pincer grasp for small objects	• More distant vision and acute hearing	• Safe household objects to explore • Blocks and stacking toys
1 year	• More mobile • May walk with help • Stands alone	• Points with index finger • Claps hands together	• Recognises familiar people, sounds and voices	• Home safety • Push and pull toys • Large balls • Lots of praise
18 months	• Walks alone • Walks upstairs 2 feet to each step	• Feeds self with a spoon • Builds a tower of 3 blocks	• May indicate toilet needs • Listens more intently	• Push along toys/walkers • Playing outside • Chunky crayons • Shape sorters
2–3 years	• Throws and kicks a ball • Runs • Walks upstairs	• Turns pages of a book • Holds pencil using a tripod grasp	• May be dry during day • Milk teeth usually complete	• Sit and ride toys • Large Duplo • Sand, water, paint • Allow time for independence
4 years	• Pedals a tricycle • Runs on tiptoe	• Threads small beads • Builds a tower of 10 blocks	• Follows the story in a book with eyes	• Dressing–up • Story books • Climbing frames • Play with other children
5 years	• Hops and skips • Dances with rhythm	• Uses a knife and fork • Fastens and unfastens buttons	• Usually dry during the night • Vision and hearing tested at school entry	• Board games • Construction toys • Creative materials • Outdoor play

Topic check

1. What do you understand by the following terms?
   - hand–eye coordination
   - developmental screening tests
   - gross motor skills
2. Explain some of the factors that can influence a child's development at any age.
3. Describe how you would encourage the fine motor skills of a 10 month old.
4. Describe the all round physical development of a 4-year-old child.
5. Give examples of toys and activities to encourage the vision and hearing of a 3-month-old baby.
6. How can good dental health be encouraged in young children?

Getting started

This topic focuses on the conditions, clothing and footwear that are needed to promote and support the physical growth and development of babies and young children. When you have completed this topic you should:

- be able to identify suitable clothing and footwear for babies and children
- understand the need babies and children have for warmth, rest, sleep, exercise, fresh air, cleanliness, routine and suitable housing.

Key terms

Cross-infection: becoming infected with something that originates from a source other than the person themselves

Nappy rash: skin rashes in the areas covered by a baby's nappy

Non-flammable: not able to burn easily

Recuperation: recovery

Regulate: control or influence

'Topping and tailing': washing a baby's face, hands, bottom and genital areas

Development conditions

Children need certain physical and environmental conditions to achieve their physical growth and development potential (see Figure 3.5). A family's lifestyle and the resources they have available to them are likely to have an effect on the physical conditions in which a child is raised.

Warmth

A warm, comfortable home environment helps a child's development. As well as being in a warm home, a baby also needs to be dressed in appropriate clothing as babies can't **regulate** their own temperature. Babies generally need to be kept warm but they mustn't get too hot either! Children also need to be warm and comfortable, but are more able to regulate their own temperature.

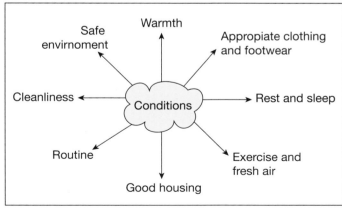

Figure 3.5 Conditions that promote physical growth and development

Rest, exercise and fresh air

Babies and children need a balance of rest and activity. Children should be encouraged to play outside so that they can get fresh air and exercise regularly. Parents can take babies and children out on wet, cold and windy days by wrapping them up in warm, weatherproof clothing and can still have fun splashing in puddles, playing in snow and using the learning opportunities provided by wet and windy weather. Going outside can provide children with opportunities to develop and practise their physical skills in the garden, at the park or playground or on the beach, for example. As children grow older, they can practise and develop their walking, running, jumping, climbing and balancing skills through outdoor play. Many parents quickly learn that lots of fresh air and exercise also give their children a good appetite and help them to sleep better too!

Routine

The arrival of a newborn baby can disrupt a family's usual routines because the baby may sleep, feel hungry and want changing at irregular times during the day and night. This can be especially difficult for the mother, who is most likely to have responsibility for feeding the baby. Establishing a feeding and sleep routine for a newborn baby becomes a priority in the early weeks and months of their life but can also be difficult to achieve. Some mothers try to introduce a regular and relatively strict feeding and sleeping timetable for their baby. Others try to adapt their own routines and focus on fitting in with their baby's natural rhythms.

Fitting in with the baby's natural rhythms can be very tiring as it may involve waking up and feeding the baby several times during the night (and during the day!) and a disrupted sleep pattern for both parents. As a baby gets older, however, a routine for sleeping, feeding, bathing and playing becomes more important and is easier to achieve. A clear, structured routine gives a child a sense of security and a sense of being cared for. Children quickly get used to routines – they become their 'normal' everyday life – though routines also have to be adapted and change as the child develops and begins new activities (like going to playgroup or pre-school) or changes their sleep pattern.

Rest and sleep

Children need regular rest and sleep to help them grow and develop. Rest and sleep allow **recuperation** of energy. Babies and children who don't get enough sleep and rest become irritable and upset. A regular bedtime routine helps a child get sufficient rest and sleep. Having a bath or wash, being read a story and hearing relaxing, soothing music can all promote relaxation and the kind of restful, secure feelings that help children go to sleep.

Some children like to have a night light on or have the door left open to reassure them at night. Others prefer not to have any light in their bedroom at all. If concerns about the dark do develop, a favourite cuddly toy or comforter can be given to the child to promote security. Parents who let their children sleep in their bed when they become anxious often regret this, as persuading their child to return to and stay in their own bed can become quite difficult.

Babies need at least 12 hours of sleep every night but may wake in the night because they are hungry or need a nappy change. As children get older, they need a bit less sleep and are less likely to wake. However, children may still need a rest or nap during the day until they are about 3 years of age, and are still likely to be sleeping for 12 hours a night at this age.

Cleanliness

Cleanliness is important for both babies and children in order to protect their skin and prevent infections. Babies and young children haven't developed the same resistance to bacteria as adults. Parents need to ensure that their own personal hygiene standards are good in order to avoid **cross-infection**. Washing hands regularly, having clean hair and keeping nails trimmed and clean all help to promote cleanliness. While a regular bath is an important way of protecting babies and young children from infection, skin irritations and discomfort, babies in particular don't need a daily bath. **'Topping and tailing'** and a bath every other day are usually sufficient.

Over to you!

Have you ever washed or bathed a baby or young child? Did you ensure that your own personal hygiene was appropriate before you began?

Bathing a baby

Bath time should be fun and enjoyable for both a baby or young child and their parents. To be successful and safe, the parent who is giving the baby or child a bath must prepare the bathroom properly and ensure that they are careful and systematic in the way they carry out the bathing. This can be achieved by doing the following:

▶ Collect together and organise all the equipment, toiletries and towels needed to bath the baby before starting to undress or wash them.

▶ Run the water and check that it isn't too hot – about 37° C – by testing it using a thermometer or with the elbow before starting to undress the baby.

▶ Undress the baby (except for their nappy) and wrap them in towels in the bathroom or close by.

▶ Before putting the baby in the bath, first wipe their face with damp cotton wool, avoiding the use of soap on the baby's skin. Remember to wipe each eye with fresh, damp cotton wool to prevent the spread of infection.

 Case study

Paula gave birth to Grace, her first child, 6 weeks ago. She was shown how to bathe and clean Grace by one of the nurses in the hospital maternity unit a couple of days after Grace was born. However, Paula hasn't given Grace a bath since she arrived home. Paula's mum has been doing this as Paula says she is 'too scared' of doing the wrong thing or dropping her baby in hot water. Paula's mum is now getting a bit frustrated with her daughter as she thinks that Paula should be bathing her own baby by now. She has asked Paula's health visitor to come and talk to Paula about this.

1. If you were the health visitor, what would you say to Paula to give her enough confidence to start bathing Grace?

2. Describe the kind of things that Paula should do to prepare the bathroom for Grace's bath.

3. How could Paula test the water to make sure it isn't too hot for Grace?

4. Make a list of the steps Paula should take to give Grace a bath safely.

▶ Wash the baby's scalp with water and a mild shampoo, rinse and then gently pat the scalp dry.

▶ Unwrap the baby from the towel. Remove their nappy, clean away any mess and dispose of the nappy hygienically.

▶ Lower the baby into the water, holding and supporting their head at the back of their neck. Wash them gently.

▶ Lift the baby out of the water and pat them dry all over, ensuring that all of the 'creases' in their skin (behind ears, joints, skin folds and so on) are completely dry.

As children get older and are more physically capable, they need less physical support to have a bath. Bath toys, encouragement to wash themselves, some bubbles and a positive attitude can then make bath time fun and exciting as well as an important part of a child's personal hygiene routine. A baby or young child should never be left unattended in the bath. Babies and children can drown in a few centimetres of water so should always be taken out if the adult in charge has to leave the bathroom for any reason.

Changing nappies

Nappy changing is an important and very frequent event in a baby's life. Both parents can be fully involved in this area of care and will quickly develop the skills needed to change nappies effectively. A soiled nappy must be changed as soon as possible to avoid irritation and damage to the baby's skin. The skin in the nappy area should be cleaned and dried each time the nappy is changed. The baby should be placed on a flat surface to change their nappy. This is to ensure that they can't roll or fall off during a nappy changing procedure.

There are lots of different techniques for changing nappies. The key to doing this effectively is to contain any mess in the nappy and then remove and dispose of it hygienically before cleaning the child's skin and putting a new nappy on. Some parents first use a baby wipe, the nappy itself or tissues to clean away mess that they find sticking to the baby's skin. The next step is to sponge the skin with warm water to clean it thoroughly. After patting this dry with a flannel or towel, a mild skin cream or zinc and caster oil can be applied to sore areas and to prevent **nappy rash**, if necessary.

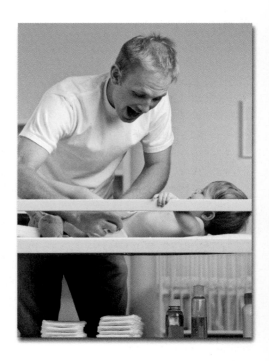

Case study

Jade, aged 17 months, has nappy rash. The skin on her bottom is very red and sore and is making her cry a lot. Jade's mum, Angie, changes her nappy first thing in the morning, just before lunch and then just before she goes to sleep at night. She doesn't wash Angie's skin unless she has soiled her nappy. This can mean that Angie has the same nappy on for several hours at a time.

1. Explain to Angie why Jade's skin is so red and sore.

2. How often do you think Jade's nappy should be changed?

3. What can Angie do to soothe Jade's sore skin and reduce the risks of this happening again in the future?

Toilet training

As they grow older, children develop bladder and bowel control and can be taught to use the toilet rather than a nappy. Girls tend to be ready for toilet training sooner than boys of the same age. Children usually learn to control their bowels before their bladder. While toilet training can begin from 18 months of age, many children require more time before they are able to cope without a nappy. Key points in relation to toilet training include:

▶ Don't rush the process – a child must be ready and interested. The child needs to be able to identify when their bowel or bladder is full and needs emptying.

▶ Provide praise and encouragement to reinforce a child's efforts to use the potty and toilet rather than their nappy. This can be quite scary for some children.

▶ Expect a child to have setbacks and accidents before they are fully confident and capable of staying clean and dry throughout the day and night.

▶ Encourage the child to wash their hands each time they use the potty or toilet and try to explain hygiene principles to them in a way they will understand.

Good housing environment

The environment in which a child grows up has an effect on their development. A child's housing environment should be safe, warm and comfortable. Damp, cramped and overcrowded conditions tend to lead to ill health and also slow or restrict a child's development. A lack of heating, stair gates, fire guards and other safety precautions can increase the risk of a child having an accident and experiencing some physical injuries. A child needs a warm, safe, secure environment to develop to their full potential.

Clothing and footwear

A wide range of clothing and footwear products are available for babies and children under 5. Parents need to consider whether clothes are:

▶ hard wearing, washable and easy to dry

▶ easy to get on and off (for the child and parent!)

▶ comfortable and loose enough for movement

▶ the right size to allow for growth

▶ suitable for the time of year and local weather conditions

▶ safe and free of hazards, such as long ties, ribbons and buttons that could be swallowed or choke a baby or young child.

A child will need clothing for different conditions and occasions. For example, they will need clothes for night time and sleeping, play time and for hot and cold weather.

Activity

Investigate the range of nappy products available. What kinds of disposable nappies are there? What do they claim to be able to do? How do the various types of nappy differ from each other? Using your findings, produce a table summarising the types of nappies available to parents of children under 5 years of age.

Over to you!

Imagine that a friend or relative has just had a baby. You know that they need baby clothes urgently and you want to buy them something as a present. What would you buy and where would you go to purchase it?

Nightwear

Night clothes must be made from flameproof materials and must be suitable for the weather conditions – cool in summer and warm in winter. They must be made from **non-flammable** materials; they need to be loose to allow movement and access for nappy changing and going to the toilet; and they should be soft and comfortable to promote sleep. It is best to avoid night clothes with ties or ribbons as these can get caught around a baby or child's neck as they move about during sleep. All-in-one sleep suits for babies and then pyjamas for toddlers and older children are ideal most of the year round. Night dresses are a cool alternative for girls in the summer, while boys can wear shorts or just underwear when the weather is very warm or hot.

Outdoor wear

Outdoor wear for babies, and especially for young children, needs to be robust and hardwearing. Clothing made from denim and corduroy is ideal and a popular choice with parents because it meets these criteria. Outdoor clothing also needs to be weatherproof to protect the child from cold and rain. Wearing a number of thin layers of clothes that can be removed or changed to suit the weather conditions is a good way of coping with variable outdoor conditions. Coats with hoods, good insulation and all-in-one suits for younger children work well in winter. Whatever clothing a child wears, it needs to allow movement but should not be so loose fitting that it gets in the way or is irritating to wear.

 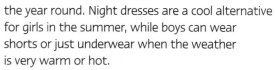 **Case study**

Nisha and Vijay will be 2 years of age in September. Meera, one of their aunties, has been wondering what she could buy them for their birthday. Their mum has suggested that she buys some outdoor clothes for the autumn and winter. Meera doesn't have any children of her own. She isn't sure what she should buy but wants to get them something 'suitable and practical'. Meera has £25 to spend on each child.

1. Describe three items of clothing that might be 'suitable and practical' for outdoor wear during the autumn and winter.

2. What criteria should Meera use when making a decision about what to buy for Nisha and Vijay?

3. What would you recommend Meera buys for Nisha and Vijay? Justify your suggestions by explaining how they are 'suitable and practical' and within the price range she can afford.

Play clothes

Many parents dress their children in particular trousers, T-shirts and tops to suit the type of play activity a child is taking part in. Clothes that are specifically for outdoor, creative or messy play need to be hardwearing, allow lots of movement and should be easy to wash. Play clothes are likely to get covered in paint, glue or other art materials or become dirty with soil and grass stains, for example.

Footwear

Babies don't need shoes. They may benefit from wearing soft booties that keep their feet warm in cold weather but shouldn't wear shoes until they are starting to walk. A child's footwear should protect their feet from bruises, grazing and hard surfaces and should keep their feet warm and dry in cold and wet weather, and cool in warm or hot weather.

A child needs to have their feet measured regularly and correctly, ideally every 3 months, so that shoes fit properly. Children's footwear needs to fit correctly to allow their feet to develop and grow naturally. A child's feet can become malformed if squeezed into ill-fitting shoes, or socks and tights that are too small and restrictive. As a result, a child shouldn't wear shoes that are too tight (even if they are fashionable or the child's 'favourite' shoes) or that belong to another child.

It is always advisable to buy children's shoes from a shop that employs specially trained fitters. A new pair of shoes should:

- have enough width/room for growth
- protect and support the child's foot
- be hardwearing.

These factors are much more important than whether the shoes are fashionable, have flashing lights or contain a secret toy compartment. The health and development of the child's feet should always be the parents' primary concern.

Over to you!

Where can parents take their children to have their feet measured by trained assistants in your local area? Ask your own parents how often you had to have new shoes between the ages of 2 and 5 years.

Case study

Oliver, aged 15 months, has just started to walk in the house. His dad is very keen for Oliver to improve his walking and would like to take him to play at the local playground. Oliver's parents have decided to buy him his first pair of shoes and some outdoor clothes this weekend.

1. What advice would you give to Oliver's parents to help them purchase a suitable pair of outdoor shoes?

2. What kinds of clothing do you think Oliver will need for outdoor play at his local playground?

3. What factors should Oliver's parents take into account when purchasing outdoor clothing for him?

Topic check

1 Identify five different features of a child's living conditions that have an effect on their physical growth and development.

2 Describe how to bath a baby, ensuring that you focus on safety and cleanliness in your description.

3 How can a poor housing environment affect a child's development?

4 Identify the main factors a parent should consider when choosing clothes for their child to wear.

5 Explain why it is a good idea to dress young children in layers of clothes rather than single very warm items of clothing.

6 What factors should a parent take into account when buying a new pair of shoes for their child?

Child safety

Getting started

This topic focuses on child safety and ways of safeguarding children from a range of hazards and risks. When you have completed this topic you should:

- be able to identify a range of hazards and risks to young children
- understand reasons why babies and young children sometimes experience accidents
- know how to reduce the risks of accidents occurring.

Key terms

British Standards Kitemark: the official mark of quality and reliability (in the form of a Kite symbol) of the British Standards Institute

Hazard: a source of danger

Non-flammable: not able to burn easily

Risk: the chance of loss, damage or injury occurring

Safeguarding: protection

Accidents and injuries to children

Parents often worry about their children having an accident and may take steps to prevent them happening. Babies and young children will always be at risk of accidents and some accidents are inevitable in every person's early childhood. However, parents should also understand the reasons for accidents so that they can do their best to prevent them occurring or minimise their impact. Accidents are the cause of a range of injuries. These can vary from minor scrapes and cuts to more disabling and even fatal injuries. As a result, parents and carers have a major responsibility to safeguard their children from **hazards** and **risks**.

Accident statistics

Accident statistics describe the type and number of accidents experienced by children. A child under 5 years of age is most at risk of having an accident in the home – especially in the kitchen or on the stairs. This is perhaps not surprising as children under 5 spend a lot of time at home.

Figure 3.6 Types of accidents affecting children under 5

Type of accident	Home	Leisure
Suspected poisoning	1,214	63
Acute overexertion	540	235
Bite/sting	356	167
Chemical affect	198	11
Crushing/piercing	1,815	525
Electric/radiation	20	13
Fall	11,200	3,693
Foreign body	1,672	317
Other/unspecified	4,872	1,686
Striking contact	136	25
Suffocation/thermal effect	1,269	86
Total	**23,292**	**6,821**
UK national estimate	477,486	139,831

Source: Adapted from RoSPA Child Accident Statistics, 2002.

Activity

Research current accident statistics for young children using the websites of the Royal Society for the Prevention of Accidents (www.rospa.com) or the Office for National Statistics (www.ons.gov.uk).

Produce a leaflet or poster describing the types of accidents younger children are most likely to experience.

Safety in the early years

Babies and infants are at risk from different types of hazards inside and outside of the home. Safety conscious parents are often very aware that their child's safety is linked to their stage of development. For example:

▶ Newborn and younger babies are unable to sit up or control their movement. As a result a baby can easily roll off a bed, sofa or raised surface (such as a changing table). Babies should never be left alone or be out of reach in these circumstances.

▶ As it grows and develops, a baby will begin to sit up and grasp objects and may put them in its mouth. Babies and young children should be carefully supervised to prevent them from choking on objects placed in their mouths.

▶ Toddlers like to crawl and climb, and may begin trying to walk from about 9 months of age. As they don't have good balance at first, toddlers may fall off furniture or down stairs, grab cables or flexes, or pull objects from surfaces around the house. All of these situations can lead to accidental injuries. Parents need to be aware of potential dangers and often reorganise the home to remove potential dangers.

▶ A child who is 3 years old is likely to have fairly good balance and will be very mobile. However, they are still unlikely to have a sense of danger. They may underestimate the risk of having a fall if they climb up or come down stairs too quickly, or they may be attracted by open windows or climb onto walls or other surfaces if left unsupervised.

▶ A 4-year-old child is much more independent and physically capable than a baby or toddler. They may be learning to ride a bike, might be able to swing on a rope or use the equipment at a local playground in an independent way, for example. However, a pre-school child will still not have a strong sense of danger and will need supervision and reminding to play safely.

In general, babies, toddlers and young children are at risk of having an accident because they:

▶ have less awareness of, and often don't understand, the dangers and hazards in everyday life

▶ don't understand the possible consequences of their actions

▶ are very curious and sometimes get themselves into dangerous situations

▶ become too excited or emotionally upset and lose focus on sources of danger

▶ are left unsupervised in a hazardous situation

▶ become physically tired and stop concentrating – late afternoon and early evening are danger periods for accidents

▶ become too boisterous or start showing off to others, forgetting about possible dangers

▶ are upset by major events or changes (e.g. illness, death, divorce, moving house) in their family and everyday environment.

Case study

Clare Marsh has two children, Liza aged 2 and Luke who is 9 months old. Liza is able to walk and can climb the stairs with assistance. Luke has recently started to crawl and seems to be able to get everywhere! He will go though open doors, crawls under chairs and tables and tries to pull himself up on furniture. He recently even crawled to the top of the stairs when Clare left him alone for a minute on the floor of his bedroom whilst she answered the phone. This frightened her. She is also worried that Liza will try to come down the stairs on her own and will fall. Clare and her partner Nick would now like to reduce the accident risks to Liza and Luke around their home.

1. Identify two different hazards that could lead to Liza or Luke having an accident at home.

2. Give two reasons why Liza or Luke may be at risk of having an accident at home.

3. Suggest three ways Clare and Nick could minimise the risks of Liza and Luke having an accident at home.

Accident prevention

It isn't possible to remove all hazards and eliminate all risks from a baby or child's life. However, many accidents are preventable and parents have a responsibility to raise their own and other people's awareness of safety risks to their children. Parents must continually assess risks to their children as these alter as their child grows and develops. It is important to appreciate a child's abilities and the extent of the hazards they face in a particular situation. Parents also have a responsibility to educate their children to understand hazards and risks to their own health and safety. This can seem like a slow process as children younger than 2 years of age don't understand the consequences of their actions and don't seem to learn the safety lessons parents try to teach them. Parents need to be especially vigilant with younger children (it is not enough to tell them to 'be careful'). Doing so will gradually lead to a child developing a sense of danger and being able to identify hazards and safety risks.

Safety at home

A child's home should be a safe environment. Parents need to identify hazards associated with different parts of the home, such as the kitchen, stairs and bathroom, and then try to minimise the risks these hazards pose to their child. For example, to minimise health and safety risks in the kitchen, it is advisable to:

▶ install and maintain smoke and carbon dioxide alarms

▶ keep electrical flexes out of reach of children

▶ store knives and other sharp utensils in a safe, secure place

▶ keep the floor dry to prevent slipping and clear of trip hazards (e.g. toys!)

▶ store plastic bags where children can't find them

▶ keep cleaning fluids and household chemicals in a secure place children can't get to

▶ ensure pans, kettles and other kitchen equipment can't be grabbed or pulled over.

Parents can also minimise risks by anticipating possible accidents and then acting to prevent them before they occur. A child's parents also need to ensure that the home

Figure 3.7 Ways of minimising accidents at home

Accident	Preventive action
Falling	Use safety gates at the top and bottom of stairs; use window catches; keep doors closed; ensure good lighting; teach safe way to climb and descend stairs; use harnesses in highchairs, prams and pushchairs
Cuts	Store knives and sharp tools in a safe place; avoid leaving knives on kitchen surfaces or tables where children can reach them; use safety glass or shatterproof film on doors and windows children might fall into or break
Electrocution	Use socket covers to stop children poking fingers or objects into electric sockets; check safety of all equipment; teach dangers of electricity; keep electrical items out of the bathroom
Scalds/burns	Check temperature of bath and sink water before washing or bathing; monitor use of hot drinks; closely supervise children in the kitchen
Poisoning	Keep all cleaning fluids in original containers in a secure safe place; keep medicines and alcohol out of child's reach; use catches and child locks on cupboards and drawers where any chemicals or cleaning fluids are kept
Drowning	Supervise children near any pool or in the bath; never leave them alone; use a non-slip mat to avoid slips and falls

environments of friends and relatives are safe and appropriate if their children visit or stay in different places without them. The diverse family lifestyles and living arrangements of others may present hazards and increase risks for children that are not present in their own home.

Activity

What kind of health and safety hazards for children are there in a kitchen?

Have a look at the cartoon of Dave's Diner, a notoriously dirty local café. Look out for possible health and safety hazards in the picture.

Using your knowledge of health and safety and accident prevention, write a letter to Dave explaining why his café is unsafe for children under five and suggest three things he could do to improve his health and safety and hygiene standards.

Health visitors and maternity units often run child first aid courses for new parents who wish to improve their understanding and skills in basic first aid. It is also advisable to have a basic first aid kit at home to deal with the minor injuries that accidents can lead to.

Hazardous substances

A child's home may contain a surprising range of substances that are poisonous and therefore hazardous to them. These include cleaning fluids, such as bleach, perfumes and aftershave, medicines, paint and glues, antifreeze and toilet cleaner. All of these substances are hazardous if swallowed. A young child may drink a hazardous substance because they like the colourful bottle or because they are just curious. A hazardous substance may contain one of the following warning symbols:

This indicates that the substance causes ill health and may damage the skin/eyes.

This indicates that the substance is a serious risk to health if swallowed or spilt on the skin.

This indicates that the substance causes burns and destroys tissue – it may also be fatal if swallowed.

If a child is seen or is suspected of drinking a hazardous substance, their mouth (only) should be rinsed with water and emergency medical help sought quickly. The child should not be given anything to drink as this might make the situation worse. The risks associated with hazardous substances can be reduced by:

▶ never leaving a child in the presence of a hazardous substance

▶ keeping household chemicals and medicines out of sight and out of reach, ideally in a locked cupboard

▶ keeping the garage and garden shed locked and any hazardous substances on high shelves or in locked cupboards

▶ never storing household chemicals in a different container to the original bottle.

Activity

What kinds of hazardous substances are present in your home? Have a look around your home and try to identify the kinds of substances that could be hazardous and harmful to a child under the age of five. Create a table like the one below to record your findings and to make recommendations about ways of improving the way these substances are stored.

Substance	How is it hazardous?	Where is it stored?	Could it be stored in a safer place?
1. Bleach	Poisonous if swallowed		
2.			
3.			
4.			

Safety outside of the home

A range of hazards exist for children outside of the home. These include hazards in the garden, on roads and at the playground.

Garden safety

Playing outside in the garden is often seen as a safe activity for young children. However, a garden may contain a range of hazards, including:

▶ plants, berries and soil bacteria that are poisonous

▶ animal excrement (from cats, dogs and birds, for example)

▶ uncovered and easily accessible ponds, pools, streams or water butts

▶ broken fences, hedges and unlocked gates that allow unsupervised children to leave the garden easily

▶ walls, fences, gates and equipment with sharp edges or rough surfaces that can cause cuts, grazes or puncture wounds

▶ rusty or broken equipment that can cause cuts, grazes or crush injuries if it falls or is pulled onto a child.

Activity

Assess your own garden or the garden of a friend or relative with children. What hazards might there be for:

1. a baby?

2. a 2-year-old toddler?

3. a 4-year-old child?

Suggest ways of reducing the risk associated with each of the hazards you identify. Present your work in the form of a short report or assessment summary.

Play equipment

Young children usually love trips to the playground. Parents and children often see playgrounds as places for adventure, activity and excitement. Boisterous and increasingly mobile toddlers and young children can use up lots of their energy exploring and using the variety of equipment playgrounds offer. Safety-aware parents also know that playgrounds contain a range of hazards, including:

▶ equipment that can hit or trap a child's limbs

▶ steps, slopes, slides and roundabouts that young children can fall off

▶ broken glass, cans, litter and animal excrement that can cause children injury and ill health

▶ larger, stronger and boisterous children who may accidently run into or push a smaller child and cause them injury.

Younger children can develop their social, emotional and physical skills by playing with others and using the equipment at a playground. However, parents must always be aware of potential hazards and need to monitor their child at all times. This doesn't have to mean interrupting their play or hovering too closely. However, it is important that parents assess and respond to potential hazards in the playground and are able to monitor their child's behaviour in order to prevent accidents happening.

Road safety

Young children have no road sense and should not be exposed to busy, dangerous roads or left alone where vehicles are moving. Young children are at risk because:

▶ they don't understand road or traffic dangers

▶ they are unable to judge the speed or distance of moving traffic

▶ they are likely to panic and act impulsively when frightened by busy, noisy traffic.

The number of road accidents and deaths of children has fallen significantly over the last 15 years. Despite this improvement, in 2008 almost 23,000 children under 16 were hurt in road accidents; 131 of these children were killed.

Figure 3.8 Road accidents involving children

Country	Fatal	Serious	Slight	All severities
England	100	2,295	16,808	19,203
Scotland	20	277	1,392	1,689
Wales	4	111	989	1,104
N.Ireland	7	94	851	952
Great Britain	124	2,638	19,189	21,996
UK (GB+NI)	131	2,777	20,040	22,948

Source: Child Accident Prevention Trust, 2009

The decline in road accidents involving young children is partly due to government road safety campaigns, such as the *Green Cross Code* and *Let's Decide Walk Wise* campaigns. These aim to reduce road accidents and promote road safety by teaching children basic road safety procedures from an early age. The introduction of child safety seats and restraints in cars and improvements in the passenger safety aspects of car design have also helped to reduce road accidents involving young children.

By law, children up to 12 years of age or 135 cm in height now have to use a safety restraint in the car. Parents now typically buy a special child seat with a restraining belt for this purpose. The type of child safety seat needed depends on the size, weight and age of the child. All child safety seats must now carry a **British Standards Kitemark**. This confirms that the seat is safely designed and made. The seat will then need to be correctly fitted and straps adjusted for each journey to ensure that it offers the level of protection a child needs.

Activity

Children under the age of 5 need close supervision near roads. Make a list of five things that parents can do to promote road safety and protect their children from danger when walking near to busy roads.

Figure 3.9 Types of child safety seat

Type of seat	Description
Rear-facing baby seat	A child's first baby seat that usually also has carrying handles and can be removed from the car. It is designed to keep the child firmly in place. Suitable for 0–9 months or up to 13 kg. Must not be used in the front of the car if air bags are fitted.
Forward-facing child seat	This seat remains in the car and is usually the child's second seat. It is suitable for a child aged 9 months to 4 years or up to 18 kg. It can be used in the front or back of the car.
Booster seat	This is designed for children aged 4–6 years. It holds the child securely and comfortably but allows them more movement and enables them to look out of the window more easily.
Booster cushion	This is a child's last safety seat. It is designed for a child aged 6–11 years. It raises them up to see out of windows while holding them securely using an adult seat belt.

Toy and equipment safety issues

Toys and other products used by children have to be safe. UK laws ensure that products produced in the UK meet minimum safety standards. The British Standards Kitemark, often found on child safety products such as stair gates, car seats and pushchairs, guarantees that the product is made of safe, suitable materials and is safe to use.

Parents should always try to buy toys that are appropriate for their child's age. This is because toys designed for older children may be hazardous to a younger child if they contain loose, removable or moving parts. All toys purchased for children should be clean, **non-flammable**, made from non-toxic materials and have no sharp edges or loose parts.

CE indicates that a toy satisfies the requirements of the European Toy Safety Directive.

The Lion Mark indicates a toy meets the safety requirements of the British Toy and Hobby Association.

 Case study

Ben, aged 2½, has three sisters who are much older than him. Ben's dad is very keen to buy his son some 'boys toys' for Christmas. He has been looking in a mail order catalogue and has identified a range of toys for Ben that he thinks are exciting and just the kind of thing that boys really love. His list includes:

- a Scalextric race track with two racing cars
- a remote-controlled helicopter
- a toy gun that looks and sounds like a real machine gun

- a climbing frame that has a 6-foot high slide and rope ladder attached to it
- a laptop computer.

Ben's mum and sisters have said that they think the list contains unsuitable toys. His dad doesn't understand why.

1. Identify two toys on the list and explain why they might be unsuitable for a 2½-year-old child.

2. What safety factors should Ben's dad bear in mind when he is choosing Christmas presents for Ben?

3. Suggest two toys that are suitable and safe for a 2½-year-old boy like Ben.

Safeguarding personal safety

Children's personal safety is increasingly a concern for parents. Worries about abuse and abduction are prevalent and are often featured in the media. Though both abuse and abduction of children are very rare occurrences, they should always be a concern for parents. Younger children shouldn't be given opportunities to wander away from their parents in public places and should not be left alone or entrusted to people their parents don't know and cannot trust. Children under 5 are unlikely to be able to protect themselves from abuse or abduction but can be taught to:

▶ never go with anyone they don't know

▶ tell their teachers and parents if they are approached by anyone

▶ wait and stand still until they are found if they become lost or separated from their parents in a busy place.

Topic check

1 Identify three types of accidents that young children experience at home.

2 Give five reasons why babies, infants and young children are at risk of having accidents at home.

3 Describe two ways of minimising accidents and injuries to infants and children in the kitchen.

4 Identify two hazardous substances present in the home and describe ways of minimising the risks they pose to infants and young children.

5 Explain why garden safety is an important issue for parents of young children.

6 Describe three ways of minimising the risk of road safety and car accidents to infants and young children.

4 Nutrition and health

Introduction

This chapter is divided into four topics:

4.1 Feeding the newborn baby

4.2 Nutrition in childhood

4.3 Food preparation

4.4 Infection and child health

This chapter is about food and its links to child development. Topic 4.1 covers a number of issues relating to the feeding and nutritional needs of newborn babies. You will learn about breast and bottle feeding as well as the process of weaning a baby onto solid food. Topic 4.2 considers nutrition in childhood in more detail, outlining the importance of healthy eating, the role of nutrients in the diet and the links between poor diet and illness. Topic 4.3 describes the importance of food hygiene and safety. You will also learn about the causes and consequences of food poisoning. Topic 4.4 describes a range of infections and their causes and explains how to recognise and respond appropriately to childhood illness.

By the end of this chapter you should be able to recognise and understand:

▶ that babies and young children have a range of nutritional needs

▶ the function and sources of the major nutrients in a child's diet

▶ the arguments for and against breast and bottle feeding and approaches to weaning

▶ the importance of healthy eating and the links between poor diet and illness

▶ how immunity to disease and infection can be acquired

▶ how to prevent, recognise and manage childhood illness

▶ the needs of sick children.

Feeding the newborn baby

▶ Getting started

This topic is all about feeding a baby during the first year of life. It examines breast and bottle feeding and the introduction of solid food for babies (the process of weaning). On completion of this topic you should:

- know about the advantages of both breast and bottle feeding
- understand the differences between breast milk and formula milk
- be able to describe how to make up a bottle feed and sterilise feeding equipment
- know about the process of weaning babies onto solid food.

Key terms

Attachment: the important emotional relationship between a baby and its adult carers (also called 'bonding')

Casein: the main protein in cows' milk

Colic: an attack of stomach pain and excessive crying in a new baby

Colostrum: the first milk produced by the mother's breasts after the birth of the baby

Express: to squeeze milk from the breasts either by hand or using a special pump

Formula milk: milk specially modified for babies

Gastroenteritis: an infection causing severe diarrhoea and vomiting

Lactation: the production of breast milk for breastfeeding

Weaning: the process of introducing solid food in a baby's diet

Breastfeeding

Breast milk is a complete food for babies during the first 6 months of life. The production of breast milk (**lactation**) is stimulated by the hormone oxytocin, which is released after the birth of the baby. This process is encouraged by the baby sucking at the mother's breast immediately after the birth. The first milk to be produced by the breasts is called **colostrum**. This substance is very high in calories and protein and also contains antibodies from the mother to protect the baby from infection. Colostrum is produced for the first few days after birth and then the breasts start to produce complete milk.

Breastfeeding uses a lot of calories. Mothers who are breastfeeding need to make sure that they eat a balanced diet, with plenty of protein, calcium and iron-rich foods.

Figure 4.1 Advantages of breastfeeding

It helps to promote **attachment** between the mother and the new baby.
It helps the mother's uterus contract back into shape.
It does not need any equipment to be sterilised, so there is less risk of the baby being infected with conditions like **gastroenteritis**.
Breast milk is nutritionally balanced for a newborn baby and easier to digest.
Breast milk is free and always available at the correct temperature.
Colostrum provides antibodies to protect the baby from infection.
Breastfed babies have less risk of being affected by allergies and conditions like eczema.

They also need to drink plenty of fluids. However, some substances can be passed directly from mother to baby in the breast milk, so alcohol and medicines should be avoided. Some of the advantages of bottle feeding are that the father, partner or other people can also feed the baby and it is easier to see exactly how much milk the baby drinks at each feed. Some mothers may choose to **express** their breast milk so that other people can feed the baby. This can be done either by hand or by using a special breast pump. The midwife or health visitor can advise the mother on how to do this. There are many factors that will influence a mother's decision to breastfeed her baby and she may have discussed some of these with her midwife during pregnancy. It may be a matter of personal choice or practical reasons, like cost.

Over to you!

Think about the decision to breastfeed a baby. What factors do you think might influence a woman's decision and why?

Bottle feeding

Bottle feeding uses **formula milk**. This is specially modified cows' milk designed for babies and is the only type of milk suitable for babies in the first 6 months of life. Ordinary cows' milk contains too much salt (sodium) for babies, which can be very harmful and can cause kidney damage. Cows' milk also contains high levels of a protein called **casein**, which is difficult for babies to digest. Formula milk is very similar in nutritional content to breast milk and there are many different varieties available. The most important factors to consider when choosing to bottle feed a baby are that:

▶ babies are cradled lovingly and held closely when feeding

▶ formula milk feeds are correctly measured and made up according to instructions

▶ all feeding equipment is thoroughly cleaned and sterilised.

Some mothers may be unable to breastfeed due to mastitis (an inflammation of the breast tissue), anxiety or because of specific medical conditions. Some formula milk comes as a ready-to-use liquid, but most comes as a powder, which needs making up into a feed. It is extremely important to follow the instructions exactly. If too much milk powder is used, the feed will be too concentrated and the high levels of sodium could be dangerous for the baby. The baby could also gain too much weight.

Figure 4.2 Instructions for making up bottle feeds

1	Clean the surface where the feed will be prepared.	
2	Wash your hands thoroughly.	
3	Make sure all feeding equipment is properly sterilised.	
4	Boil water and leave it to cool.	
5	Pour the correct amount of cooled boiled water into the feeding bottle.	
6	Check the amount of water is at the correct measure on the side of the bottle.	
7	Measure the exact amount of milk powder as recommended on the instructions using the scoop provided. Add into the feeding bottle.	
8	Carefully place the teat and cap onto the bottle and shake gently.	
9	Cool the milk quickly by holding under cold running water or placing the bottle in a container of cold water.	
10	Check the temperature of the milk by shaking a few drops onto the inside of your wrist. It should feel lukewarm, not hot.	

Activity

Investigate a variety of different formula milk products available at your local supermarket. Produce a chart to summarise the different kinds available and their cost.

Sterilising feeding equipment

It is extremely important to sterilise all feeding equipment used with babies in the first year of life. This is to prevent infections like gastroenteritis, which can be very dangerous and even life threatening for babies. The different ways of sterilising feeding equipment include:

- sterilising solution (chemical method)
- electric steam steriliser
- microwave steriliser.

Instructions for sterilising equipment should always be followed carefully and all the equipment used for preparing feeds should be sterilised.

Feeding safety

If instructions are carefully followed for making up formula feeds and sterilising feeding equipment, then a bottle-fed baby will thrive. However, there are some important points to remember.

Figure 4.3 Safe bottle feeding practice

DO	DO NOT
Hold the baby closely when feeding.	Prop the bottle up against a pillow or leave the baby alone when bottle feeding.
Make sure the hole in the teat is not blocked or too large.	Feed the baby too quickly.
Throw away any milk that is left in the bottle at the end of the feed.	Reheat any formula milk that is left in the bottle after a feed.
Make up feeds one bottle at a time.	Use any milk feed that has been left at room temperature and not been used within 2 hours.
Store the made up bottle feed in the fridge (if it is not going to be used immediately).	Keep any milk in the fridge for longer than 24 hours.
Warm feeds if necessary using a bottle warmer or standing the bottle in hot water.	Use a microwave to warm bottle feeds.

Feeding routines

Feeding time is always special whether a baby is breast or bottle fed. It should never be rushed and is a time when the parent and baby can enjoy being close. Babies should always be cradled during feeding time and parents should make eye contact, talk softly or stroke the baby's cheek. This is very important for developing the attachment relationship between the baby and the parent.

Babies often swallow air when they are feeding and this can lead to them developing wind. Pausing during feeding can help the baby to bring up wind. Holding the baby up against a shoulder and rubbing the baby's back gently can also help. Sometimes, babies can experience a condition called **colic**, which can be very uncomfortable and causes the baby to cry for long periods. It usually settles down in the first few months of life as the baby's digestive system matures.

Newborn babies will generally be fed on demand, that is when they are hungry. This can sometimes mean as many as ten feeds during the day and night. Most babies will soon start to settle into a feeding routine and usually by about 3 months, the baby will not need feeding during the night.

Activity

Investigate the different methods of sterilising feeding equipment. Create an information leaflet for parents outlining the advantages and disadvantages of each method.

Case study

Rosa and Dominic's baby Anton is 8 weeks old. Rosa has been breastfeeding Anton since birth but is planning to return to her part-time job in 2 weeks' time. Anton will be cared for by a childminder when Rosa is at work and sometimes by Dominic. Rosa still intends to carry on breastfeeding although she would like to introduce some bottle feeds for Anton during the day.

1. What advice would you give to Rosa about bottle feeding?

2. Make a list of the equipment she will need.

3. What could be some of the advantages of bottle feeding for this family?

Weaning

Weaning is the process of introducing solid food into a baby's diet. Milk provides all the nutrients a baby needs for the first 6 months of life but as the baby grows, a more varied diet is needed. Solid food should always be introduced very gradually. Babies are born with a natural reflex to suck, but the action of chewing has to be learnt and this should not be rushed.

When to start weaning

Most babies will start to show signs that they are not satisfied with just a milk feed. The baby might:

▶ still be hungry after a milk feed

▶ wake up hungry during the night (when it usually sleeps through)

▶ demand to be fed more often.

Six months is the recommended age to start weaning. Research tells us that starting solid food too early can be harmful for babies. Solid food is much more difficult for babies to digest and contains more salt (sodium) than milk. Starting solid food too soon can also lead to the baby developing some allergies.

The health visitor will provide help and support for parents during this important stage of infant feeding.

How to start weaning

The process of weaning should always be introduced gradually. Very small amounts of food should be offered to the baby using a plastic teaspoon, which can be sterilised.

The food needs to be similar in consistency to milk to begin with and mixed into a smooth puree. This should be offered just once a day, as the baby will still be having milk feeds regularly. Gradually the amount of solid food given to the baby will increase. A wider variety of foods can be offered as the baby gets used to chewing and feeding from a spoon. Babies enjoy touching their food and mealtimes can get very messy!

Step by step babies can be given the same food as the rest of the family and will enjoy feeding themselves with a spoon or with their fingers. They will also start to drink from a feeder cup, although they will probably still have a breast or bottle feed before bedtime. It is very important never to leave babies alone while feeding as they can easily choke.

Figure 4.4 Stages of weaning

Stage of weaning	Consistency of food	Suitable examples	
First (from about 6 months)	pureed	baby rice mixed with breast or bottle milk; carrot, banana, lentils	
Second (about 6–9 months)	mashed finger foods	potato, cooked apple, dhal, yoghurt, carrot sticks, pitta bread, rusks	
Third (about 9–12 months)	chopped	meat, fish, pasta, rice, beans	

Weaning foods can be prepared very easily for babies by mashing or liquidising fruits, vegetables or pulses. This is one way to ensure that weaning foods are nutritious and offer variety for the baby. Salt should never be added to weaning foods as this can be harmful for the baby's kidneys. Sugar should not be added as this can affect the baby's developing sense of taste. There is also a wide range of ready prepared weaning foods on the market, such as baby rice, savoury meals and desserts. These foods vary from jars and packets to tins and cartons. Their nutritional content is strictly controlled and clearly labelled, and many parents find these products very convenient to use as part of their baby's weaning diet. It is important for babies to experience a variety of different foods to encourage healthy eating patterns.

 Over to you!

What do you think are the advantages and disadvantages of using ready prepared weaning foods for babies? In pairs or small groups, make a list of your ideas.

 Activity

Investigate a range of weaning foods available at your local supermarket and make a chart to present your findings. Highlight a range of products for each stage of weaning, the type of product (e.g. packet, jar, tin) and the cost of each one.

The importance of milk

As the baby starts to eat more solid food, the amount of milk feeds given will gradually decrease. Some babies will drink cooled boiled water as an alternative. Babies still need about 600 ml of milk every day until at least 12 months of age and this should continue to be either breast milk or formula milk. Ordinary cows' milk should not be given to babies until they are at least a year old. When cows' milk is offered, it should not be skimmed milk until the child is 5 years old, although semi-skimmed can be given from the age of 2 years. It is also recommended to give children vitamin supplements from the age of 1 to 5 years. The health visitor will provide help and guidance for parents.

Activity

What advice about feeding would you give to parents in the following situations?

1. William is 6 months old and has been fully breast fed since birth. During the past week, he has started waking up in the middle of the night, chewing on his fist and crying. What advice would you give?

2. Helena is 7 months old and has been eating small amounts of baby rice at lunchtime for the past 2 weeks. She seems to enjoy this and her mother is anxious to try some different foods. What would you suggest and why?

3. Karina is 9 months old and enjoys a wide range of mashed-up food at lunch and teatime. She loves to feed herself with her fingers and her parents are looking for ideas for different finger foods to try. What would you suggest and why?

4. Oliver is 12 months old and enjoys most family foods. He can feed himself with a spoon (although this is usually a bit messy!). His mother is worried about what kind of milk to give him and how much he needs. What would you advise?

Mealtimes as a social occasion

It is very important to encourage babies to be part of the family at mealtimes. Even from an early age, babies can sit in a highchair at the family table and enjoy being included. Mealtimes are important for babies to learn self-help and social skills, such as being part of a group, developing independence and learning to communicate their needs. They will also enjoy playing with their food so it is always a good idea to protect the floor with a washable mat!

Case study

Rosa and Dominic's baby Anton is now 7 months old and he started weaning 3 weeks ago. So far, he has enjoyed baby rice mixed with formula milk and pureed apple, pear, carrot and potato. He also likes to hold his own finger foods, such as breadsticks. Rosa still gives him a breastfeed first thing in the morning and before he goes to bed at night.

1. Plan a full day's meals for Anton, including breakfast, lunch and tea. Give examples of suitable weaning foods for each meal.

2. What advice would you give Rosa and Dominic about continuing to wean Anton over the next few months?

Topic check

1 What are the main advantages of breastfeeding?
2 Describe the process of making up a bottle feed.
3 What are the main differences between breast milk and formula milk?
4 Explain the main ways to sterilise feeding equipment.
5 Describe the process and stages of weaning.
6 Why should sugar or salt not be added to a baby's food?

Getting started

This topic is all about healthy eating in childhood. It explores how to encourage healthy attitudes towards food and the importance of healthy eating patterns for young children. It also examines some diet-related issues, including food intolerance and medical conditions. On completion of this topic you should:

- understand the importance of healthy eating for young children
- know about the major nutrients and main food groups
- know about diet-related illnesses.

Key terms

Attention deficit hyperactivity disorder (ADHD): a condition involving problems with concentration and overactive behaviour

Diabetes: a disease with high levels of sugar in the blood

Food intolerance: a reaction to a food or ingredients in a food product

Food refusal: refusing to eat food offered at mealtimes

Nutrients: substances contained in food that provide nourishment for growth

Obesity: the condition of being extremely overweight; more than 20% above the ideal body weight

Weaning: the process of introducing solid food in a baby's diet

Developing healthy eating in childhood

During the process of **weaning**, a wide variety of foods should be offered to the baby. This helps to develop the baby's experience of different foods and encourages the baby's sense of taste. Healthy eating habits can be developed from a very young age and parents should encourage sensible eating patterns and healthy food right from the start.

Figure 4.5 Encouraging healthy eating with young children

Offer a variety of different foods.
Always encourage children to try different foods, even just a small amount.
Enjoy family mealtimes together.
Encourage regular mealtimes with children, rather than 'snacking' between meals.
Cook and bake with young children and encourage them to enjoy eating what they make.
Go shopping together and include children in making choices about food.
Grow food in the garden or planters and encourage children to help.
Have fun with food and make mealtimes interesting.
Avoid fizzy drinks and processed or 'fast' food, and offer healthier options instead.
Seek advice from the health visitor or family support worker.

A healthy diet

Food contains **nutrients** that are essential for good health. Macronutrients are nutrients that are needed in large amounts, like protein and carbohydrate. Micronutrients are the vitamins and minerals that are needed in smaller amounts, but are still an important part of healthy eating. A healthy diet contains a balance of these important nutrients, which all perform a different function in the body.

Figure 4.6 What goes in to a healthy diet

Macronutrients	Function in the body	Example foods
Protein	growth and repair of body tissue	meat, fish, milk, cheese, eggs, soya, beans, pulses
Carbohydrate (starches and sugars)	to provide energy	starch: bread, potatoes, pasta, rice sugar: sugar, sweets, chocolate
Fat	to provide warmth and energy	butter, cream, cheese, eggs, olive oil, nuts
Fibre	helps digestion and prevents constipation	fruit, vegetables, wholegrain cereals and bread
Vitamins (micronutrients)		
A	healthy skin and eyes	oily fish, green vegetables
B group	healthy nervous system	wholegrain cereals and bread
C	protection against infection	citrus fruits, green vegetables
D	helps the body to use calcium	oily fish, eggs, natural sunlight on the skin
Minerals (micronutrients)		
Iron	healthy red blood cells	red meat, green vegetables
Calcium	strong bones and teeth	milk, cheese, yogurt, green vegetables, nuts

Healthy eating

Most foods contain several nutrients, for example milk contains protein, fat, vitamin B and calcium. When planning meals it is important to include foods that contain a balance of all the essential nutrients. This is vital for young children who are growing quickly and have high energy levels. Freshly prepared food with plenty of fruit and vegetables, wholegrain cereals and starchy food like pasta will provide young children with the essential nutrients they need for good health. Children should be encouraged to drink water, milk or unsweetened juice rather than fizzy, sugary drinks.

Processed foods like hot dogs and ready prepared meals can be very high in fat, sugar and salt. It is important to read the labels on these foods and only use them in moderation with young children. Some prepared foods like baked beans or fish fingers can be combined with fresh food as part of a balanced diet.

The Food Standards Agency has developed the eatwell plate, which shows the different types of foods that make up a healthy diet. This provides a complete guide to food selection and healthy eating.

Diet-related issues

There are many factors that may influence a child's diet, including:

- parental choice or lifestyle
- child's age and stage of development
- religion or cultural differences
- food intolerance or allergies
- specific illnesses or medical conditions.

Vegetarian and vegan

Some parents choose to be vegetarians or vegans and may want their children to follow similar eating patterns. Vegetarians do not eat any meat or fish and vegans do not eat any animal products, including eggs and cows' milk. Soya and other sources of plant protein are therefore very important. If children follow a vegetarian or vegan diet, then special care will need to be taken to make sure all the essential nutrients are included in their diet.

Religion and culture

Some religions and cultures have strict guidance about what kinds of food should be eaten and even how animals should be killed. For example, Jews do not eat any meat from a pig (pork, bacon, ham) and most Hindus do not eat any meat at all. Islamic (Muslim) law requires meat to be ritually slaughtered (halal meat).

Food intolerance

Some children may have a reaction to certain foods or food ingredients. This is called **food intolerance** and it can result in problems for young children. Food allergies are a type of intolerance and foods that commonly cause allergies with young children are cows' milk, wheat and eggs.

The symptoms of a food allergy can include vomiting, diarrhoea, stomach pain and skin rashes. Most children grow out of food allergies as they get older, but parents need to be very careful about the ingredients in different foods and should always check food labels carefully. Some specialist food products are available for children with food intolerance and allergies, for example soya milk for children with cows' milk intolerance.

Diet-related illness

The food that children eat affects their health and wellbeing in both the long and short term. Many health problems and medical conditions are diet-related and these can be prevented if healthy eating habits are established with children from an early age. Children who eat food that contains more calories than they use in energy will put on weight. If this pattern continues it can easily lead to **obesity**. Obesity can cause problems in the short term as it becomes more difficult for obese children to be active. It can also cause more long-term problems, as overweight children are more likely to develop conditions like **diabetes** later in life. Obese children often grow into obese adults and this only adds to their long-term health problems, with a greater risk of conditions like heart disease and high blood pressure. Children can also experience deficiency diseases caused by a shortage of some nutrients in their diet. For example, rickets is a deficiency disease which can be caused by a lack of calcium in the diet, and anaemia is a deficiency disease caused by a lack of iron.

Diet and dental health

Too much sugar in the diet can be very harmful to children's teeth. Bacteria in the mouth react with the sugar to form acid. This attacks the tooth enamel and causes decay. Natural sugar is present in many foods, such as fruit, but it is the sugar added to food that is the most harmful to children's teeth. Foods with high levels of added sugar include tinned fruit in syrup, sweet fizzy drinks and flavoured jelly. Children should be given low-sugar snacks, like fresh fruit and breadsticks, and should limit sweet foods like biscuits and cake. Water and unsweetened juice are much healthier alternatives to fizzy, sugary drinks.

Activity

Investigate a range of food products in your local supermarket. Check the labels carefully and list all the ingredients in each product. Which products would not be suitable for a child with:

1. cows' milk intolerance?
2. an allergy to eggs?

Activity

Use the internet, library or other resources to investigate Type 2 diabetes. Design an information leaflet or web page that outlines the major causes of this condition and how eating healthily can help to prevent it.

Over to you!

Why do you think young children like sweet foods so much?

Think about different ways to encourage healthier eating options for children.

Diet and development

As children develop more independence they can become more fussy about what they eat. This can result in **food refusal** (not eating their food). It is a developmental stage that most children go through but it can be a very worrying and frustrating time for parents.

Figure 4.7 Reasons why children refuse their food

They are starting to practise their independence and saying 'no'.
Food may not be the most important thing on their mind; they would rather be playing.
Their appetite will vary depending on how active they have been during the day; sometimes they will eat a lot and some days hardly anything at all.
They may enjoy the attention from their parents when they refuse food.

Children rarely become ill because of food refusal. All children are individuals and are developing their own likes and dislikes. They may like a particular food one week, but will refuse to eat it the next. Parents need to be patient during this phase and should continue to offer attractive, nutritious meals at regular mealtimes. Sweets and snacks should not be given to children between meals. Children will eat when they are hungry, but if parents are really concerned then they should ask the health visitor for advice.

Children's diet can also have an influence on their behaviour. Conditions like **attention deficit hyperactivity disorder (ADHD)** have been linked to food additives such as colourings, artificial flavourings and preservatives. Children with ADHD have difficulty concentrating and their behaviour is often hyperactive. Research has shown that limiting foods with lots of additives can improve the behaviour of some children with ADHD.

Activity

Plan a healthy, balanced meal, including drinks, for the following children:

1. a school lunchbox for Jamie, aged 5 years, whose parents want him to be vegetarian

2. dinner for Parveen, aged 3 years, who is a Muslim

3. breakfast for Ana, aged 18 months, who has a cows' milk intolerance.

List all the nutrients you have included and give reasons for your choices.

Topic check

1   What do you understand by a healthy, balanced diet for young children?

2   Describe some of the ways that children can be encouraged to eat healthily.

3   What are the main nutrients contained in food?

4   Give examples of some common food intolerances in young children.

5   What are some of the health problems that obese children can face?

6   Describe two diet-related illnesses that can develop later in life if children do not eat healthily.

Food preparation

▶ Getting started

This topic is all about the importance of hygiene when preparing food for young children. It explores the causes of food poisoning and other infections and how to prevent cross-contamination. On completion of this topic you should:

- know about the importance of hygienic practices when preparing and storing food for children
- understand how food becomes infected
- be able to prevent cross-contamination when preparing food for children.

🔑 Key terms

Bacteria: microscopic organisms that can cause disease

Cross-contamination: the spread of bacteria from raw, contaminated food to other food

Dehydration: excessive loss of water from the body

E-coli: bacteria that can cause food poisoning

Food poisoning: illness caused by eating contaminated food

Gastroenteritis: a stomach infection caused by bacteria, with symptoms of extreme vomiting and diarrhoea

Salmonella: bacteria that can cause food poisoning

Toxins: poisonous substances produced by bacteria

The importance of hygiene

Good hygiene practice is very important when preparing food for babies and young children. Infection can spread easily if strict hygiene procedures are not followed. Babies and young children have very little resistance to infection and are vulnerable to conditions like **gastroenteritis**. Personal hygiene is crucial in preventing the spread of infection.

Personal hygiene

▶ Always wash your hands before touching food, after using the toilet or handling anything dirty.

▶ Cover any cuts with waterproof plasters.

▶ Do not cough or sneeze over food.

Children should also be taught good hygiene habits from an early age. They should be encouraged in routine hand washing before meals or snacks, after using the toilet and following any messy or outdoor play.

Over to you!

Think about the different ways young children can be encouraged to develop good hygiene habits.

How food becomes infected

Food can become infected with harmful **bacteria**. Bacteria are organisms that can multiply rapidly and produce **toxins** (poisons). These toxins can cause **food poisoning** and other dangerous illnesses. Bacteria grow and multiply in conditions where there is warmth, moisture and food. Hygienic food preparation and storage helps to limit the growth of bacteria. Some key points are:

▶ always keep food covered

▶ keep food in the fridge at a temperature between 0° C and 5° C

▶ always cook food thoroughly (heat destroys bacteria)

▶ never reheat food more than once

▶ keep all food preparation surfaces clean

▶ always use clean utensils and dishcloths

▶ empty kitchen rubbish bins regularly

▶ keep pets out of the kitchen

▶ always check 'use by' dates on food products.

Some of our food naturally contains bacteria that are not harmful, for example yogurt and cheese. However, the bacteria found in raw food, particularly meat, can be harmful unless is it destroyed by thorough cooking. Raw meat should always be stored and prepared with great care.

One of the most common ways for food to become infected is by **cross-contamination**. This is when bacteria from raw contaminated food spread to other food. For example, if the juices from a raw joint of beef in the fridge drip onto some cooked ham on the shelf below.

Bacteria can also spread and contaminate food through the use of utensils, for example using the same knife to cut up raw chicken and then make sandwiches, without cleaning the knife in between.

Preventing cross-contamination

The best ways to prevent cross-contamination of food are by practising strict hygiene rules when preparing and storing food. Some key points are:

▶ use separate utensils and chopping boards for raw meat and cooked foods

▶ always wash knives and other utensils thoroughly after cutting raw meat

▶ always keep raw food covered in the fridge

▶ store cooked food above raw food in the fridge

▶ always wash your hands thoroughly between handling raw and cooked foods.

Activity

Design a simple information leaflet or web page for parents, explaining the importance of hygienic food storage and preparation, and the dangers of cross-contamination.

Over to you!

Carry out an assessment of your own kitchen at home. Make a list of the positive and negative features relating to food hygiene.

Food poisoning

One of the most common causes of food poisoning is from **salmonella** bacteria found in raw chicken and raw eggs. It is very important that chicken and eggs are cooked thoroughly in order to kill these harmful bacteria. Soft-boiled eggs (with a runny yolk) should not be given to children in the first year of life. Food poisoning can also be caused by **E-coli** bacteria, which normally live in the intestines, but can be very harmful to babies and young children. The main symptoms of food poisoning are vomiting and stomach pains, and symptoms can start within just a few hours of eating contaminated food. Babies and young children have very little resistance to these bacteria and can become seriously ill. There are strict legal guidelines about the storage and preparation of food for manufacturers and retailers. If these regulations are not followed, there can be serious outbreaks of food poisoning and severe health risks to the public.

Gastroenteritis is a serious illness that can be life threatening for babies. It is caused by bacteria that infect the stomach and produce symptoms of severe diarrhoea and vomiting. It is more common in bottle-fed than breastfed babies because of the risks involved with the preparation of formula feeds. Babies with gastroenteritis can very quickly develop **dehydration**, which is a serious condition for babies and often requires hospitalisation.

Activity

Imagine you are a food hygiene inspector about to visit the home of a childminder who cares for two children, aged 6 months and 3 years.

Write a checklist of all the food hygiene measures you would be looking for in the kitchen or other areas where food is prepared and stored.

Topic check

1 Describe the key elements of good personal hygiene when dealing with food.
2 Explain three important points about the safe and hygienic storage of food.
3 Give examples of how cross-contamination can be prevented.
4 What are some of the main causes of food poisoning?
5 What is gastroenteritis and why can it be so dangerous for babies and young children?
6 List some of the important food hygiene measures in a kitchen where food is prepared for babies and young children.

Infection and child health

Getting started

This topic is all about illness in young children. It examines how to recognise some of the common childhood diseases and how to care for a sick child, including preparation for a stay in hospital. It also covers how infection can be spread and the importance of immunisation. On completion of this topic you should:

- ☑ understand how infection is caused and how it can spread
- ■ know about the common infectious diseases of childhood
- ■ understand how children develop immunity to disease
- ■ be able to recognise childhood illness
- ■ know how to care for a sick child and when to seek medical help
- ■ know how to prepare a child for a stay in hospital.

Key terms

Antibodies: specialised proteins created by the body's immune system to fight off infection

Asthma: a non-infectious condition that can be triggered by allergic reactions and causes breathing difficulties

Chicken pox: an infectious disease caused by a virus that produces very itchy spots

Convulsion: uncontrollable contraction of muscles in the body causing jerking movements

Febrile convulsion: a convulsion caused by a high body temperature (above 39° C)

Head lice: parasites that can live on the human scalp

Immune system: the body's defence system against infection

Immunisation: boosting the immune system by injection with vaccines

Incubation period: the time taken for symptoms to appear after becoming infected with a disease

Meningitis: a serious infectious disease affecting the meninges around the brain and spinal cord

Parasites: living creatures that feed on the human body

Regression: going back to an earlier stage of development or behaviour

Symptoms: changes in the body caused by an illness

Child health

There are many factors that help to keep a child healthy. Eating a nutritious, well-balanced diet, being out in the fresh air and getting plenty of exercise and sleep are all very important in preventing illness. Good hygiene also helps to prevent illness in young children. Simple measures like hand washing, covering the mouth when coughing or sneezing, and using tissues (which can be thrown away) all help to prevent the spread of infection. A healthy child will have a good appetite, enjoy being active, sleep well, gain weight and make normal developmental progress.

Childhood illness

Most children will experience some episodes of illness in their life. Some illnesses, like coughs and colds, are not usually serious and can be dealt with by the parents. Some, like **meningitis**, are more serious and will need specialist medical care. Illnesses like **chicken pox** are infectious (easily spread) and some, like **asthma**, are not infectious at all.

Young children find it difficult to describe how they feel. They may say that they have 'tummy ache' when they actually feel upset, afraid or worried. Children's **symptoms** can worsen very quickly and they should always be taken seriously and not ignored.

Causes of illness

The main causes of illness in young children are:

▶ infections – caused by bacteria or viruses, for example coughs and colds

▶ genetic – caused by genes that children inherit from their parents, for example haemophilia (a bleeding disorder)

▶ external – caused by environmental and lifestyle factors, for example allergies.

Infectious illnesses

Infectious illnesses are caused by bacteria or viruses and are spread easily. Some of the common infectious diseases in childhood include coughs and colds, measles and chicken pox. Bacteria and viruses spread mainly in the air (droplet infection) or through direct contact with an infected person (touching them or things they have used). When bacteria or viruses infect the body, they multiply quickly and produce symptoms. Symptoms are changes in the body caused by the infection, for example an increase in body temperature or a rash. Once children are infected, they can easily pass on the infection to others. This can happen even before the symptoms appear, during the **incubation period** of the infection. For example, a child with chicken pox will be infectious and can pass on the infection to others for several days before the spots even appear. This is one of the reasons why childhood illnesses can spread so quickly.

Figure 4.8 The main signs of illness in a child

Poor appetite
No energy
Change in behaviour (unusually quiet, not sleeping well, crying more than usual)
Constipation or diarrhoea
Vomiting
Skin rash
Raised body temperature
A cough, headache, stomach ache, earache or runny nose
Not gaining weight

Over to you!

In pairs or small groups, make a list of all the childhood illnesses you can think of. Include serious and non-serious conditions, infections and other illnesses.

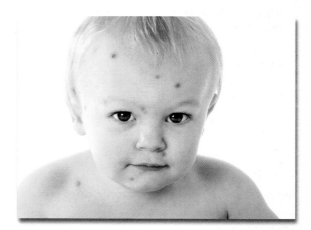

Activity

Use the internet, library or other resources to investigate these common infectious diseases of childhood:

• measles
• mumps
• rubella (German measles)
• chicken pox.

Make a chart that shows the main symptoms of each disease, how it should be treated and how long each one is infectious for.

Most infectious diseases start with symptoms like a bad cold, with a slight rise in body temperature, a sore throat and generally feeling unwell. Some infectious diseases also produce specific symptoms including a rash. With chicken pox the rash usually appears within 24 hours. The spots are red and raised and very itchy. Children should be prevented from scratching the spots which will eventually blister and form crusts. Measles produces a rash which is dark red and blotchy. The spots usually start on the face and neck and then spread to the rest of the body. Children with measles can be very sensitive to bright light and their room should be kept dark and quiet. Rubella (German measles) is often quite a mild infection, but the child may have a rash of pinkish spots and swollen glands in the neck. Mumps causes a sore throat and swelling on one or both sides of the jaw which can be painful for the child when chewing or swallowing.

Infected children should always be seen by a doctor, who will prescribe any necessary treatment. It is important for infected children to have plenty to drink, even though they may not feel like eating much. Children should also stay away from nursery or school until they are no longer infectious and the doctor says they can return. Children will recover completely from most of the common infectious diseases within a few weeks. Some infectious diseases, like meningitis, are more serious. Meningitis can be caused by either bacteria or a virus and it affects the meninges, the protective covering around the brain and spinal cord. The most common symptoms of meningitis are headache, neck stiffness and a high body temperature. It can also cause a blotchy skin rash, which does not fade under pressure, and this is usually a serious sign of the disease. The child should always see a doctor if meningitis is suspected. It can be a life threatening condition and the child may need to be admitted to hospital.

Immunity

Good health helps children protect themselves from infection as their **immune system** develops and matures. The immune system is the body's natural way of fighting off infection and other diseases. It takes a few years for the immune system to fully develop, which means that babies and young children are very vulnerable to infection. Children can be protected from some infectious diseases through routine **immunisation**. Immunisation boosts children's immunity by producing **antibodies**, which help to fight off infection. A routine programme of immunisations is offered to all children through the National Health Service. Immunisations are usually given at the child health clinic or GP surgery and parents are notified when their child's immunisations are due. Protecting children through immunisation has resulted in diseases like diphtheria and polio being very rare in the UK.

Activity

Use the internet, library or other resources to investigate these infectious diseases:

- polio
- diphtheria
- tetanus
- whooping cough.

Find out about the symptoms of these diseases and how they used to threaten the lives of young children years ago. Present your findings in the group.

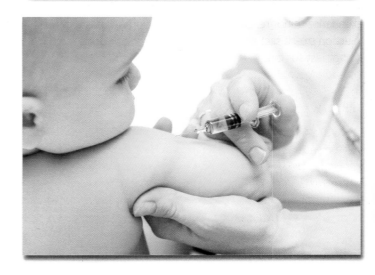

Before immunisation was available, these diseases used to kill large numbers of children every year. It is important that parents continue to have their children immunised so that these diseases do not become common again.

Figure 4.9 Routine immunisation programme for children aged 0–5 years

Age given	Immunisation against (vaccine given)
2 months	Diphtheria, tetanus, pertussis (whooping cough) **(DTaP)**, polio **(IPV)** and Haemophilus influenzae type b **(Hib)**, which can cause meningitis Pneumococcal infection **(PCV)**
3 months	Diphtheria, tetanus, pertussis (whooping cough) **(DTaP)**, polio **(IPV)** and Haemophilus influenzae type b **(Hib)** Meningitis C **(Men C)**
4 months	Diphtheria, tetanus, pertussis (whooping cough) **(DTaP)**, polio **(IPV)** and Haemophilus influenzae type b **(Hib)** Meningitis C **(Men C)** Pneumococcal infection **(PCV)**
Around 12 months	Haemophilus influenzae type b **(Hib)** Meningitis C **(Men C)**
Around 13 months	Measles, mumps and rubella **(MMR)** Pneumococcal infection **(PCV)**
3 years and 4 months (or soon after)	Diphtheria, tetanus, pertussis (whooping cough) **(DTaP)** and polio **(IPV)** Measles, mumps and rubella **(MMR)**

Figure 4.10 Non-routine immunisations

Age given	Immunisation against
At birth (to babies at risk of TB)	Tuberculosis **(BCG)**
At birth (to babies whose mothers are Hepatitis B positive)	Hepatitis B **(Hep B)**

Risks and reactions

Most immunisations are injected into the child's upper arm or thigh. Some children experience minor reactions to immunisations including swelling and redness at the injection site, a slight rise in temperature or just being a bit irritable. These reactions do not last for long and are usually nothing to worry about. Very occasionally children will experience more serious reactions to immunisation and parents should always seek advice from their GP. In most cases, immunisation produces a life-long immunity to these diseases.

There are very few reasons why a child should not be immunised. Children are much more at risk from infectious diseases than from immunisations. If a child has certain allergic conditions, fits or convulsions then the parents should discuss this with their GP or health visitor before the child is immunised.

Over to you!

What do you think about routine immunisation for children?

Should all children have to be immunised or should parents have a choice?

Activity

In small groups, design a short TV advertising campaign that would encourage parents to have their children immunised.

Parasites

Some conditions in children are spread by **parasites**. Parasites are living creatures that live and feed on the human body. **Head lice** are the most common parasites that affect children. Head lice live on the scalp and can spread very easily between children, particularly in schools and nurseries. They lay eggs (called nits), which can sometimes be seen as white specks in the hair. Special treatment is needed to remove head lice and parents should check with their GP, health visitor or chemist.

 Activity

Use the internet, library or other resources to investigate head lice and other common parasites that can infect children.

Find out about the symptoms produced by different parasites and the treatment that would be needed in each case. Create a chart to summarise your findings.

Non-infectious illnesses

Some illnesses are not infectious but can still cause health problems for young children. Conditions like earache, stomach upsets and diarrhoea are often experienced by children, particularly once they start mixing with other children. These are usually not serious unless they continue without improvement and then a doctor should always be consulted.

Asthma is a non-infectious condition that causes breathing difficulties for children. It can be triggered by allergic reactions to materials like pollen or animal fur. Asthma can be very successfully managed and treated with specific medicine from the doctor. This is sometimes taken by the child using a special inhaler. Many children grow out of this illness as they get older.

Caring for sick children

Children can be very miserable when they are sick. Normally children enjoy being active and busy and they dislike having to stay in bed or not being able to play. Most children recover very quickly from illness, but it is important to know when medical or emergency help may be needed.

General care of a sick child

Being ill can be a frightening experience for young children and they need lots of attention with plenty of hugs and reassurance. They may be comfortable on the sofa downstairs or in their own bed with a favourite blanket or special teddy. The room should be warm and well ventilated but not draughty. Sick children often do not want to eat much, so meals should be small and appetising. It can be a good time to be indulgent with the child's favourite treats! The child should also have plenty to drink, especially water, but it is a good idea to avoid fizzy drinks. Sick children have less energy and so will enjoy quiet play activities like looking at picture books or having stories read to them. As they start to get better, they will enjoy doing more with activities like jigsaws or crayoning.

 Over to you!

Can you remember being sick as a child? What happened to you?

Share your memories in groups and compare your experiences.

Taking a child's temperature

Normal body temperature is usually around 37° C. Any rise in body temperature is usually a sign of illness in a child (sometimes called a fever). A very high temperature (above 39° C) is usually a sign of a serious illness and a doctor should always be contacted.

There are several ways to take a child's temperature.

A forehead strip thermometer

This plastic, heat-sensitive strip is placed against the child's forehead. The strip changes colour to give the body temperature reading. It is not as accurate as a digital thermometer.

Forehead strip

A digital thermometer

This is very easy to use and can be placed under a baby's arm or in a child's mouth. The body temperature is shown clearly on the digital display.

An ear thermometer

This is a type of digital thermometer that is used directly in the child's ear. It gives an accurate reading on the digital display.

Note: clinical (mercury) thermometers should never be used with babies or young children. They are made of glass, easily broken and mercury is poisonous.

Digital thermometer

Reducing a high temperature

A high body temperature can be dangerous in young children. In some cases it can lead to a **febrile convulsion**, which can be life threatening. If a child's temperature rises to 39° C or above, then a doctor should always be called. There are some general measures that can be taken to reduce a child's high temperature, including:

▶ sponging or bathing them in lukewarm water

▶ removing their clothing and any blankets or other bedding

▶ using a fan to cool the room temperature

▶ giving the child plenty of drinks of water

▶ giving the recommended, measured dose of liquid paracetamol (but not to babies under 6 months old).

Ear thermometer

Activity

Visit your local chemist or supermarket and investigate some of the over-the-counter medicines that are sold for children with a high temperature.

Use ICT to make a chart that shows:

- the name of the medicine
- the age range of children it is suitable for
- the dosage that should be given
- any special instructions.

Giving medicines to children

Generally, medicines should only be given to young children on the advice of a doctor. It is always important to follow instructions carefully and only give medicines that are appropriate for the child's age. Children's medicines are usually in a liquid form because tablets can cause choking. Medicine should be given to children using a clean plastic spoon and should always be measured carefully. A dropper or small plastic syringe can be used with babies. Medicine should never be given to a child in their food or drinks because it will not guarantee that they get the correct dose.

Figure 4.11 Safety with children's medicines

Always store medicines in a safe place, locked away and out of the reach of children.
Never give more than the recommended dose of the medicine.
Always complete the full course of the medicine, even if the child's symptoms seem to be better.
Never give other people's medicine to children.
Always throw away any out of date medicine as this is no longer effective.

When to call the doctor

A child's condition can improve very quickly but it can also worsen very quickly. It is important to know when to call the doctor or get emergency medical help.

Medical help should always be called when a child has:

▶ a high temperature of 39° C or above

▶ breathing difficulties

▶ a convulsion or fit

▶ become unconscious

▶ very severe or constant diarrhoea and/or vomiting

▶ a purple/red rash that doesn't fade under pressure

▶ swallowed anything dangerous, for example medicine or bleach.

 Case study

Jamie is 3 years old and has chicken pox. His mother has contacted the doctor who advised that Jamie will be infectious for about a week, until the spots have dried up and scabbed over. The doctor suggested that Jamie should stay at home until then and should be prevented from scratching his spots. Jamie is miserable because he has to stay indoors and he wants to play with his friends. His spots are very itchy and he does not feel like eating anything.

1. What advice would you give Jamie's parents about caring for him at home, physically, emotionally and socially, while he is sick?

2. What signs should his parents look out for that might suggest Jamie's condition was getting more serious?

Children in hospital

There will be times when babies or young children need to go to hospital. This may be as an emergency, for example because of an accident or severe infection such as meningitis. It could also be a planned admission for an operation or medical care for a long-term condition like diabetes.

Hospitals can be frightening places for young children. It is difficult for children to be in a strange environment with a routine that is different from the one they are used to. Hospitals are also very busy places and children will see lots of new, unfamiliar people. It might also be the first time the child has ever been away from home and they could also be in pain. Sometimes children are admitted to hospital as an emergency, in which case there will be very little time to prepare them for the experience. If children know that they are going into hospital, it is important to involve them in the preparations. This can help them to feel more in control of the situation and less anxious or worried.

Over to you!

Have you ever been in hospital? What do you remember about the experience?

Have you ever visited anyone in hospital? What was that like for you?

Share your memories in groups and compare your experiences.

Preparing for a stay in hospital

There are lots of things that parents can do to help prepare their child for a stay in hospital, including:

- visit the hospital beforehand so the child knows what it is like
- share books, stories or DVDs with the child about going in to hospital
- talk to them about what will happen and take time to listen and answer their questions
- encourage the child with small-world play or role-play about going into hospital
- support the child in packing their own bag and remember to include favourite toys or special comfort objects.

Most children will only need to stay in hospital for a short time. With some more severe illnesses children may need a longer stay. Any illness can affect a child's development, but a long stay in hospital can cause **regression**. Regression means going back to an earlier stage of behaviour or development. For example, a 5-year-old child who never usually wets the bed at night could start to do this after a severe illness or a long stay in hospital. Regression is not permanent and once the child is fully recovered he or she will return to normal developmental progress.

The importance of play

Play is very important for sick children. It helps them to understand what is happening and can make things feel more normal. Play can be a helpful distraction for sick children and take their mind off feeling uncomfortable or bored. It might also help to prevent them from scratching those itchy spots! Sick children usually cannot concentrate for very long and do not have much energy. Quiet games and activities that do not need children to think too hard can be helpful, especially if children have to spend time in bed. They may enjoy old toys that they have not played with for a long time. Play can also be a very useful way to prepare children for going into hospital. Toy medical kits and playing at 'being the doctor' are practical ways that children can prepare themselves for the experience.

Activity

Investigate a range of toys and activities that would be useful for a 4-year-old child who is going into hospital. Present your findings in the group.

Look up information from the organisation *Action for Sick Children*. Use this to design an information leaflet or web page for parents about preparing their child for a stay in hospital.

Topic check

1 Explain the main ways that infection can be spread among young children.
2 What are the main signs of illness in a child?
3 Describe the needs of a sick child.
4 List some of the key symptoms that would be a sign that emergency medical help should be called.
5 Explain the importance of immunisation for young children.
6 Describe how to prepare a 4-year-old child for a stay in hospital.

5 Intellectual, social and emotional development

Introduction

This chapter is divided into five topics:

5.1 Conditions for intellectual development

5.2 Patterns of intellectual development

5.3 Emotional development

5.4 Social development and behaviour

5.5 Play

Overall, this chapter introduces you to the processes of intellectual, social and emotional development that children experience between birth and 5 years of age. Topic 5.1 describes the range of factors that influence intellectual development in early childhood. You will also consider how babies and young children can be encouraged and supported to learn. Topic 5.2 outlines the pattern of intellectual development, also known as developmental 'norms', that children follow in their first 5 years. Topic 5.3 changes the focus to children's early emotional development, but also provides an account of

developmental norms and factors that influence emotional development. Topic 5.4 focuses on the conditions needed for social development, social development norms and the links between social development, parental discipline and children's behaviour. Topic 5.5 is the final section of the chapter. This focuses on the important role of play in children's intellectual, social and emotional development.

By the end of this chapter you should be able to recognise and understand:

▶ that children's intellectual development is influenced by a range of nature and nurture factors

▶ that intellectual development follows a pattern that leads to the development of communication, language and numeracy abilities

▶ that the development of a child's social skills and behaviour are closely linked to emotional development and parenting

▶ that children learn and develop socially and emotionally through different types of play.

Conditions for intellectual development

▶ Getting started

This topic focuses on the range of conditions and factors that are needed to promote intellectual, social and emotional development in childhood. When you have completed this topic you should:

- understand how nature and nurture factors can stimulate a child's development
- be able to identify examples of nature and nurture factors
- be able to describe how a child's intellectual development can be stimulated.

🔑 Key terms

Attachment relationship: an emotionally close relationship with a parent or carer through which an infant develops and expresses their emotions and sense of security

Cognitive: related to thinking skills and mental processes, like remembering and problem-solving

Genes: the basic biological unit of inherited ability

Impairment: the loss, lack or absence of some kind of ability

Intellectual: something involving the use of the mind

Nature: biologically-based factors or influences

Nurture: factors or influences that are based in the person's external environment

Intellectual development

Learning to think imaginatively, solve problems, use language and remember are all examples of **cognitive** or intellectual skills. They all rely on a child developing and using their mind or mental abilities. Children experience a lot of **intellectual** development in their early years of life because they are constantly learning new things about the world and the environment they are in. Children learn to understand and use concepts (ideas) as they find out about the world around them. A child's understanding of time, numbers, colours and the difference between light and dark, day and night all rely on them learning these concepts.

Nature and nurture

A child's intellectual development is influenced by the **genes** they inherit from their parents and the environment in which they are brought up. These two factors are sometimes described as **nature** (genes) and **nurture** (environmental) influences.

The nature-nurture debate has been discussed by practitioners in medical, education and childcare professions for many decades. Some people believe that a child's natural abilities inherited from their parents have a more powerful influence on their development, while others believe that it is the quality of a child's environment that is the most important factor affecting their development.

People who see nurture as a key factor argue that stimulating a child by reading stories, playing lots of games, talking to them and providing lots of activities can affect the extent and rate at which they develop intellectually.

The nature–nurture debate is ongoing and is likely to remain unresolved. A child's intellectual development is likely to depend on the genes they inherit but also the level of stimulation, encouragement and opportunities they have to use their potential. To maximise their learning and intellectual potential, every child requires:

▶ a secure, loving and trusted **attachment relationship**

▶ confidence that their basic physical needs (food, safety and sleep, for example) will be met

▶ opportunities to talk and communicate with adults and other children

▶ toys, books and activities that stimulate them to explore, try out and experience objects, problems and new activities.

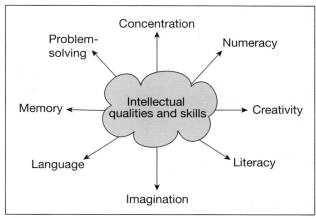

Figure 5.1 Intellectual qualities and skills

Case study

Younis, aged 4, knew the alphabet and could count to 20 before he went to school. He could also identify colours, different shapes and had a very good vocabulary. Younis's mum, Farzannah, is a primary school teacher but spent the first 4 years of his life at home, looking after him. Younis's dad, Ali, is a GP. Both of Younis's parents read a lot at home and buy lots of books and educational toys for him. As Younis is their only child, he also gets lots of personal attention and always seems to be playing or talking with one of them.

1. Identify one nature factor and one nurture factor that could explain Younis's intellectual development.

2. Describe how Younis's parents promote his intellectual development.

Stimulating intellectual development

Babies and toddlers are very curious and are keen to learn about the world around them. In the early weeks, months and years of life a child will use all five of their senses to explore and try to make sense of their environment. For example, babies and young children use:

▶ sight to identify and look at new objects, especially colourful and shiny things that attract their attention

▶ taste to test and try to understand edible and inedible objects, placing toys, clothing and other small objects in their mouth

▶ touch to explore, stroke and hold new objects

▶ hearing to develop their awareness and knowledge of the people and things around them

▶ smell to identify their mother.

Parents often purchase toys for babies and toddlers that are specifically designed to stimulate one of the five main senses. Rattles, mobiles, noise-making toys and dolls or teddies are designed to stimulate a baby or young child to hold, shake and look at them, for example. You may have seen, or might even remember, the kind of toys and mobiles that are used on cots, cradles and prams to stimulate a child's curiosity and intellectual development. In the early stages of learning, a child's senses are critical to their learning. Children with sensory **impairments**, such as hearing impairment or eyesight problems, may learn at a slower pace because they are less able to learn through one of their senses.

Activity

Imagine that a close friend of yours had her first baby a month ago. You are going to visit and see her for the first time since the birth. When you ask her about buying a present for the baby, your friend suggests a 'suitable toy to stimulate him'.

Using catalogues or the websites of shops that sell baby toys, identify toys that are designed to stimulate the senses of a young baby. When you have reviewed the purpose of each toy, choose the one that you think would stimulate the baby's intellectual development best.

Strategies for learning

As they grow and develop, children use a number of different learning strategies. Each of these strategies promotes their intellectual development.

Exploring

Babies and young children make use of the movement skills that they have to explore the world around them. Babies will reach, grasp, roll and later crawl towards objects, people and places that interest them. Parents and carers can stimulate a child's learning by offering and placing toys, teddies and other objects around a child's cot or the room where they are playing. This is a way of encouraging the child to explore and gain information and helps them to understand their world a little bit more.

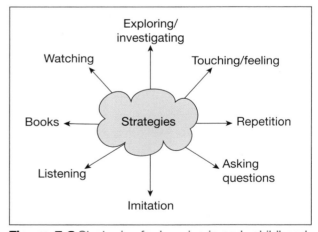

Figure 5.2 Strategies for learning in early childhood

Repetition

Babies and young children quickly become very good at looking at and listening to adults, the television and radio and other children as a way of learning about them. Often children want the same game, story or nursery rhyme to be repeated so they can learn and remember it. When they are playing, toddlers may also repeat the same activity over and over (opening and closing a dolls house door, for example) as a way of learning something about the world. Repetition helps the child to develop

Case study

Elliot's dad gets a bit exasperated when Elliot says 'again, again' each time he finishes reading him a story. Sometimes Elliot's dad has to read him the same story 5 or 6 times in a row before he will be allowed to stop. Elliot knows exactly what happens in most of the stories that his dad reads and gets upset if his dad skips a page or tries to cut the story short! Elliot's dad is now wondering why his son does this and whether there might be something wrong with him.

1. What would you say to Elliot's dad – why does his son want stories repeated?

2. Is Elliot's need to have stories repeated a sign that something is wrong with him?

3. How is Elliot's dad promoting his son's intellectual development?

their knowledge and understanding, and builds up their memory and recall skills. Being able to remember and recall information is important for later learning.

Imitation

Babies and young children imitate or copy what they see and hear in the environment around them. This can help them to develop their language skills as they imitate (without really understanding) simple words or sounds made by their parents or siblings. Similarly, copying other people's behaviour helps the child to learn how to behave in different situations (eating at the table, sitting in a chair, using the toilet). 'Let's pretend' role-play games also involve imitation and can help the child to understand the roles that other people play within the family (as 'mum' and 'dad', for example) and in wider society (as a 'policeman', 'nurse' or 'hairdresser', for example).

Activity

Watch a couple of television programmes that are aimed at young children under the age of 5. Try to identify ways in which the programmes encourage learning through:

- repetition (e.g. repeating sounds or actions)
- through imitation (e.g. 'let's pretend' activity or dressing up).

Make some notes as you watch the programmes. Using your notes, describe an example of the way one of these television programmes used one of these strategies to encourage children's learning.

Looking at books

Children can learn a lot of language skills from sharing books with adults. Many parents, grandparents and siblings enjoy reading books with their children. Local libraries, playgroups and pre-school nurseries also provide books and 'story time' activities to encourage children to read and learn through books.

Picture books, children's nursery rhyme books and short stories can all be used to stimulate a child's language skills, concentration and general curiosity. Babies and younger children may be stimulated by soft, tactile books that they can hold, feel and press. As well as offering stimulation through different textures and colours, these books sometimes also play sounds that attract the child's interest. As a child develops more language skills, the words and the story in a book become more important. Reading books and encouraging children to remember or read sections themselves helps to stimulate their listening, concentration and language skills in a sociable and enjoyable way.

Asking questions

Learning to speak is a key feature of intellectual development during infancy. Children do not actually use their first proper words until they are about 1 year old. By the time they are 2 years old most children will point at and name familiar objects when they see them ('dog' or 'bus', for example) and be able to join a few simple words together ('go park' or 'shoes on', for example). However, most children don't begin asking questions or using longer sentences until early childhood. By about the age of 3, children begin asking lots of questions. These 'how', 'what', 'why' and 'who' type of questions are designed to provide them with as much information about the world as they can obtain! Though they can seem to be never ending, parents and care workers should try to answer a child's questions as clearly and patiently as possible.

Who helps children to learn?

Parents and any carers, such as childminders or playgroup and nursery staff, have a very important role in promoting a young child's learning and intellectual development. Each of these people can provide opportunities for the child to learn through stimulating, encouraging and supporting them through a range of play activities. At home this might involve reading to the child and playing games with toys, dolls or other objects, as well as talking and explaining things to the child. Childminders, playgroup and nursery staff, and people who work in pre-school settings have to implement the Early Years Foundation Stage (EYFS) curriculum, which focuses on learning basic literacy and numeracy skills (see Chapter 6 for more on the EYFS).

Activity

Go to the website of the National Literacy Trust (http://www.literacytrust.org.uk/database/eyfs.html) if you want to find out more information about the Early Years Foundation Stage Curriculum. Summarise the background to the EYFS and find out what children are expected to be able to do by the ages of 3, 4 and 5.

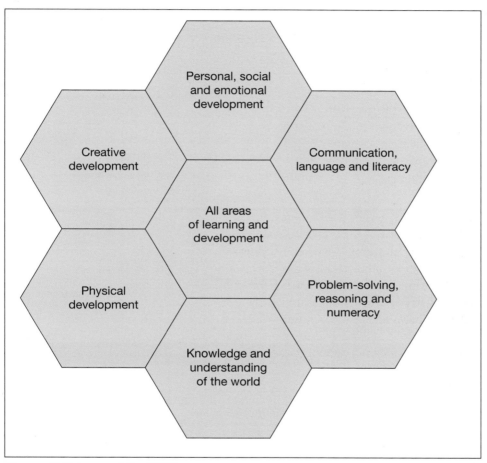

Figure 5.3 Areas of the EYFS

Topic check

1 Identify three things that change as a result of intellectual development.
2 Give an example of one nature factor and one nurture factor that can influence a child's intellectual development.
3 Describe how newborn babies learn about their environment.
4 How does looking at books and listening to stories help young children to develop intellectually?
5 Who helps young children to learn and develop intellectually?
6 What does the Early Years Foundation Stage curriculum focus on?

Patterns of intellectual development

Getting started

This topic focuses on children's early learning. It introduces you to stages of intellectual, or cognitive, development and the literacy and numeracy skills that are learnt during childhood. When you have completed this topic you should:

- know that a child's intellectual development progresses through different stages of learning
- be able to describe key features and patterns of early learning.

Key terms

Bilingual: the ability to speak two languages

Cognitive: the scientific term for 'the process of thought'

Grammar: the rules used to form words and make sentences

Hearing impairment: full or partial loss of hearing, which may be temporary or permanent

Mimicking: copying or imitating somebody

Patterns of learning

A child's intellectual development progresses through a sequence of stages that are marked by 'milestones' or developmental norms.

Figure 5.4 Intellectual development during early childhood

Age	Developmental change
Birth	A baby explores, using their senses to learn.
1 month	A baby is able to recognise their parents or main carers by sight and smell.
3 months	A baby learns by playing with their hands, holding and grasping objects.
6 months	An infant is aware of their parent or carer's voice and can take part in simple play activities.
9 months	An infant recognises familiar toys and pictures, joins in games with familiar people and is able to respond to simple instructions.
12 months	An infant can copy other people's behaviour and is able to use objects (e.g. brush or spoon) appropriately.
15 months	An infant can remember people, recognise and sort shapes and knows some parts of body ('Where is your nose?').
18 months	An infant is able to recognise themselves in a picture or reflection, can respond to simple instructions and is able to remember and recall simple information.
2 years	A child can complete simple jigsaws and develops a basic understanding of the consequences of their actions.
2½ years	A child is now usually very inquisitive, asking lots of questions, knows their own name and can find details in pictures.
3 years	A child can usually understand time, is able to recognise different colours, can compare the size of different objects (bigger, smaller) and is able to remember the words to their favourite songs and rhymes.
4 years	A child can usually count to 20, has a much better memory, can draw simple pictures of people and is able to groups objects ('all the square red blocks') together.
5 years	A child can now usually draw detailed pictures of people and objects, use their imagination, observations and knowledge to act out adult roles and is beginning to read and write.

Numeracy

Children begin developing their numeracy (number) skills from an early age. They often don't realise that they are learning about numbers because numeracy concepts are 'hidden' in the conversations, stories and songs, for example. As a result, numeracy learning is quite informal and begins with a child developing an awareness rather than an understanding of numbers.

A child's numeracy develops further from about the age of 3. A child then develops the ability to match numbers to objects ('Can you see four frogs?') and know numbers have an order ('What comes after 6?'). Children gradually develop the ability to understand and apply more complicated numeracy concepts, such as size, mass and volume, in early childhood. Play activities using water, sand, beakers, buckets and measuring jugs are often used in pre-school and infant school settings to promote the development of these numeracy concepts.

Drawing

Young children are typically quite enthusiastic about drawing and painting pictures. Children's drawings progress from simple squiggles and scribbles to more controlled circles and lines. This progression relies on the development of the child's fine motor skills. As these skills improve, the child is able to manipulate their pencil, pen or crayon more easily. At the same time, the child's intellectual abilities are developing so they learn to add details (e.g. eyes, nose, mouth) to their drawings and keep progressing (e.g. adding arms and legs) until they are able to represent people and objects in quite a clear and meaningful way.

Language development

An individual's language development begins at birth. Babies can communicate as soon as they are born, even though they can't speak. A baby will very quickly learn to use a variety of non-verbal methods of communication. For example, a baby will use crying, facial expression, body movement and eye contact, as well as pointing and touch to communicate their needs and feelings.

Learning to talk

A baby will gradually move from using non-verbal to verbal forms of communication. A baby will make sounds and gradually learn how to control and repeat them. A baby's language development is helped by:

▶ people talking to them
▶ listening to music and voices singing
▶ **mimicking** and copying sounds
▶ practising their own speech.

 Over to you!

Can you think of a game or activity that encourages children to use or develop their language skills? Singing nursery rhymes is an example of this. Can you think of any others?

Parents and pre-school workers have an important role to play in stimulating a child's language development. Parents and other adults can help by:

▶ talking to the child, repeating words and phrases that are new or difficult

▶ listening, encouraging and rewarding the child's efforts to speak

▶ being patient by giving the child time to choose and say words

▶ answering questions the child asks in a patient, informative way

▶ reading stories, and singing nursery rhymes and songs.

Other factors that affect the pace of language development include:

▶ gender – boys' language development tends to be slower than girls'

▶ developmental focus – if a child is concentrating on learning to walk, for example, their speech may be delayed

▶ lack of opportunity – this can occur where a sibling 'talks for' the child, giving them less chance to practise their own speech

▶ lack of stimulation – this can occur in families where people just don't talk to each other very much

▶ disabilities – a child with a **hearing impairment**, learning disability or a physical ability that affects their **cognitive** development may experience slower and more limited language development.

Stages of language development

A child's language development progresses through a sequence of stages that are marked by 'milestones' or developmental norms (see Figure 5.5). Infants acquire a better understanding of the world around them quite quickly as they begin to explore their surroundings and interact with their main carers. By the time they are 2 years old most children will point at and name familiar objects when they see them (e.g. 'dog' or 'bus') and will be able to join a few simple words together (e.g. 'go park' or 'shoes on'). However, while most children don't begin asking questions or using longer sentences until early childhood, the environment in which an infant lives can influence the speed and extent to which they develop intellectually. Stimulation, support and encouragement are all important features of this early learning.

Activity

Observe a child under the age of three, either on work placement or after gaining the consent of the child's parent(s). Focus on the child's use of language. Make a note of the different ways in which they communicate (verbally and non-verbally). Find out what they are able to say (if anything), when they started to speak or use their voice to communicate and what their parent or care providers think about their language ability. Create a language profile of the child you observe (protecting confidentiality) and compare this to those created by your class colleagues to assess how children of different ages develop their language skills.

Figure 5.5 Language development during early childhood

Age	Developmental change
Birth	A baby communicates through physical movement (e.g. by moving their arms and legs), by crying and through eye contact.
1 month	A baby begins to make gargling sounds, will look at people to get their attention and interacts by making 'cooing' sounds.
3 months	A baby will smile and make noises to communicate with familiar people and will cry loudly to express discomfort or hunger.
6 months	An infant can now make a number of speech-like sounds (e.g. 'goo', 'der', 'dhah' and 'ka'), will 'talk' to themselves by babbling and looks for source of sounds they hear.
9 months	An infant can now use basic sounds to say simple words e.g. 'dada' and 'mama'.
12 months	An infant can follow simple instructions and can use simple words such as "bye bye".
15 months	An infant now has enough language to join in with nursery rhymes and songs and enjoys having stories read to them.
18 months	An infant will babble simple sentences and can respond to simple questions and more complex requests and instructions.
2 years	A child can make two word sentences ('dog gone'), understands lots of words and can name familiar, everyday objects.
2½ years	A child can think of and ask questions and is able to recall and repeat familiar rhymes and songs.
3 years	A child is able to make and say longer sentences to describe what they see and express their feelings ('I'm a bit cranky today'), can hold a simple conversation, is able to use about 200 different words and can learn more than one language if they live in a **bilingual** family.
4 years	A child's language is now much more fluent. They can describe events accurately, tell jokes and can hold a short conversation.
5 years	A child is usually a fluent and confident talker, is able to use **grammar** correctly, shows an interest in new words and the use of language, and is beginning to read and write.

Topic check

1   What should a baby have learnt to do by the time it is 3 months old?
2   When does a child first start to understand the consequences of their actions?
3   Describe how children develop their numeracy abilities.
4   What can a child's parents do to promote their language development?
5   Outline the reasons why some children learn to speak and understand language more slowly than others.
6   Explain the general pattern of language development that occurs between 6 months and 2½ years of age.

Getting started

This topic focuses on the conditions that promote emotional development during infancy and childhood, and the stages of development that children go through. When you have completed this topic you should:

■ understand the importance of attachment and bonding for emotional development

■ know about the factors that influence emotional development during infancy and childhood.

Key terms

Attachment: a close personal relationship between a parent and child

Bonding: a strong feeling of connection towards another person

Regression: returning to a former emotional state

Separation anxiety: a feeling of strong anxiety and abandonment

Sibling: a brother or sister

Socialisation: the process of learning the behaviours, attitudes, values and way of life of a society

Early emotional development

Emotional development during infancy is extremely important. A baby and their parents should establish an emotional link, based on strong feelings of love and affection, during the first days of the baby's life. This process of emotional linking is known as **bonding**.

Bonding is important for both the baby and their parents. A child who has a strong bond with their parents should be able to develop feelings of trust and security during infancy. This will enable them to go on to form satisfying friendships and relationships with other people during childhood and later life. Parents who bond with their child want to shower their baby with love and affection and have a strong urge to nurture and protect them. It is the strong emotional bond with their baby that causes parents to get up in the middle of the night to feed and comfort them, for example. Babies who have a strong bond with their parents feel more secure and develop stronger self-esteem than babies who don't. A child who doesn't develop a strong emotional bond may fail to thrive both emotionally and physically.

Some parents bond instantly with their baby. This is often the case where the mother is given her baby to hold as soon as they are born. Direct physical contact and eye contact between mother and baby help to promote a strong physical bond. For others, the process of bonding takes a bit longer. This is especially the case if the baby requires intensive care and physical

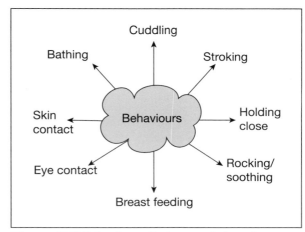

Figure 5.6 Behaviours that promote bonding

contact is initially limited. However, most parents do bond with their baby as a result of everyday care-giving. Holding the baby closely and securely during feeding, providing comfort when they are upset and soothing them when they are unwell or uncomfortable all contribute to the bonding process. The positive feelings parents get from seeing their baby's first smile or when they notice how the baby responds positively to a cuddle are points at which many parents realise how strongly they have bonded.

Attachment

The emotional bond between a baby and their parents develops into an **attachment** relationship in the first year of life. The quality of the relationship between a baby and parent is influenced by:

▶ how sensitively the parent understands and responds to the baby's needs
▶ the personality of the parent or carer
▶ the consistency of the care that the baby receives
▶ the baby's own temperament.

Figure 5.7 Signs of attachment

Age	Signs of attachment
3 months	Baby cries to get parent's attention – response is comforting.
4 months	Baby cries when parent leaves the room – needs reassurance to stop crying.
6–8 months	Infant is anxious about strangers – wants more kisses and cuddles.
9–10 months	Infant regularly checks parent is still in the room – looks up when playing.
18 months	Infant becomes clingy and is reluctant to be parted from parent – relies on parent being around for reassurance.
3–4 years	Child become more independent – can be separated from parent (e.g at nursery) if reassured that parent will return.
4 years	Child more independent – can be left with familiar people without anxiety developing.

Separation anxiety

Many young children experience **separation anxiety** in the first few years of life. This is a natural thing that can be managed and which will reduce as the child gets older, grows in confidence and has the experience of being cared for by grandparents, trusted friends of their parents or child care workers. Going to playgroups, using babysitters (relatives or trusted people) and inviting other parents and children to play at home are all ways of helping a baby or toddler to overcome separation anxiety.

Factors affecting emotional development

A child's emotional development is influenced by a range of nature (biological) and nurture (environmental) factors (see Figure 5.8). A child's home circumstances, the parenting style they experience and their life experiences generally are key features of their 'environment'.

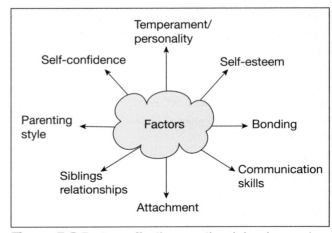

Figure 5.8 Factors affecting emotional development

Case study

Yasmin, aged 2, is looked after at home by her mum Julia and her dad Mike. Julia gave up work when Yasmin was born and thinks it is important that she is there to provide care for her daughter. Yasmin has never been looked after by or left with anybody else and has only recently started going to a playgroup on a Friday.

Julia and Mike both accompany Yasmin to the playgroup and keep a close eye on her. This isn't difficult because Yasmin doesn't really like playing with the other children. She stays very close to her parents and looks anxious when they move away or encourage her to go and use the toys and play equipment. Mike is a bit worried that Yasmin is frightened of other children and is wondering why she seems to lack confidence.

1. How would you explain Yasmin's behaviour at playgroup to her parents?

2. What do you think Yasmin might be worried about?

3. What could Mike and Julia do to help Yasmin gain in confidence?

A child is able to develop emotionally when they:

▶ feel loved and experience affection from their parents and carers

▶ are given opportunities to learn and receive support to become more independent

▶ are valued as individuals

▶ are praised for acceptable behaviour

▶ receive reassurance and support to become self-confident

▶ feel secure in relationships with other people.

A child's parents should try to:

▶ be positive and consistent in the way they respond to and care for their children

▶ meet their children's emotional needs in supportive ways

▶ provide a secure relationship for their children.

Emotional development problems

The process of early emotional development usually involves a child experiencing some setbacks and losing some of their self-confidence. In most cases this is a temporary setback that can be overcome by parents who are loving, affectionate and supportive. However, problems with early emotional development can also result in some children developing behavioural and relationship problems. A child who feels insecure, for example, may also develop low self-esteem and feel unwanted and unloved. As a result, the child may struggle to develop, express or control their emotions. The child's insecurities might be expressed through:

▶ aggressive behaviour

▶ shyness

▶ attention-seeking behaviour

▶ rudeness

▶ jealousy

▶ aggression.

Regression

A child who 'regresses' goes backwards to an earlier stage of emotional development. They might, for example, start to wet the bed at night again, refuse to use the toilet or return to eating with their fingers rather than using cutlery. Children regress when they feel emotionally vulnerable or threatened. In this kind of situation a child's parents need to be calm, patient and supportive with them. It is important to talk to the child about any worries they may have and to try out different ways of dealing with them. Being angry, upset or critical of a child will not result in improvements or get them to 'behave properly' again.

Being frightened

During infancy and early childhood, children often develop fears (e.g. of the dark, animals, 'monsters' or noises) that they find disturbing and distressing. A child's developing imagination and lack of knowledge about things like 'monsters' and the dark can exaggerate these fears and the sense of threat. In situations like this, a child needs comfort and reassurance to prevent their anxieties growing. At the same time, it is important to avoid reinforcing the child's fears by being too concerned or giving them too much attention. Many children benefit from the use of a comfort blanket or a soft toy from which they obtain reassurance at night.

Sibling relationships

Sibling rivalry is the term given to competition or jealousy between brothers and/or sisters. This can develop where one sibling in a family feels left out or that they are treated in a less favourable way to their brothers or sisters. Parents sometimes notice sibling rivalry developing when a new baby arrives in a family. An existing child or children can feel that the new baby is getting more attention and may express their jealousy by becoming more:

▶ clingy towards their parent(s)

▶ aggressive and easily upset

▶ withdrawn and less talkative

▶ selfish and less willing to share or help

▶ regressed and 'baby-like' in their behaviour and speech.

Parents can prevent and deal with sibling rivalry by:

▶ avoiding any kind of favouritism – ensuring fair and equal treatment

▶ involving existing children in the care of the new baby

▶ being affectionate and giving time to each child

▶ talking about and explaining what sibling relationships should involve.

Stages of emotional development

A child's emotional development can't be separated from social, language and intellectual development. Emotional development and **socialisation** are clearly linked, for example. During infancy and early childhood, children have to learn to control their emotions. Initially, children struggle to control their temper and may shout and cry in response to frustrations, for example. With parental guidance and support a child gradually learns more appropriate ways of expressing these feelings. Being in control of their feelings and the way they express themselves enables a child to build and maintain relationships in a socially acceptable way.

Children pass through a number of different stages of emotional development. The key milestones ('norms') of emotional development are presented in Figure 5.9.

Figure 5.9 Emotional development milestones

Age	Development milestone
Birth	A baby uses simple body movement, cooing sounds and facial expression to express pleasure. Babies cry when they are uncomfortable, frustrated or in need of attention (e.g. wet or hungry).
1–2 months	A baby begins to express their personality, using sounds and non-verbal communication to show when they are calm, excited and content, for example.
3 months	A baby may show enjoyment of routines such as bath time by giggling, squeaking and kicking their legs when pleased. At this age, babies often make cooing sounds and 'shouting' noises to show they are happy.
4–5 months	A baby will smile at other people and is learning new facial expressions to express their emotions.
6 months	An infant will become shy with strangers and is likely to cling to one of their parents or carers for security. They are also able to smile, laugh, cry, coo, use body language and squeal to express their growing range of emotions.
9 months	An infant is able to express anger, may use comfort toys, develops a stronger fear of strangers and sometimes 'separation anxiety' when their mother leaves them. At this age infants also begin to express their likes and dislikes (e.g. for food, clothes, TV programmes).
12 months	Infants seek attention and reassurance, and show affection for familiar adults. They cuddle up to parents, can become fearful (e.g. of vacuum cleaner, loud noises) or angry if their toys are taken away or they are frustrated by something or somebody.
15 months	An infant is likely to be more co-operative now but also has temper tantrums. Mood swings can occur rapidly and frequently.
18 months	Infants are starting to show greater independence and express emotions more strongly. An infant's frustrated rage and temper tantrums can seem quite alarming and powerful!
2 years	A child may still have frequent temper tantrums but is becoming more inquisitive about their environment and other people by this age. Language development is helping the child to express their feelings.
2½ years	A child may become fearful (e.g. of the dark or people they don't know), and express strong emotions because of frustration and insecurity but tantrums are usually easing as their speech improves. They may also become irritable due to tiredness, hunger and boredom.
3 years	A child is now able to be caring towards others, and is more independent and emotionally stable. Some children are now calmer though others still struggle with strong emotions. Some children become very confident while others are fearful and insecure at times.
4 years	Children now express a lot of emotions through 'let's pretend' play. They may have a strong will and an emerging sense of humour. Extreme emotions are sometimes expressed when a child talks about 'loving' or 'hating' something or someone, for example.
5 years	Children are usually able to empathise with and show sympathy for others, can cope for longer without parents (e.g. at school or playing at friends' houses) and have stronger 'likes' and 'dislikes'. In general, children are calmer and more in control of their emotions.

From the moment a child is born, their parents start learning how to communicate with them. Parents become skilled at recognising the sounds and non-verbal strategies used by their child. Parent–child communications improve quite rapidly and become detailed and complex.

As they grow and develop, a child's emotions go through periods of being stable and unstable, with quite rapid changes occurring at times. These periods of emotional stability and instability are caused by the physical changes, environmental influences and relationship changes a child is experiencing. Parents need to be calm and sympathetic to changes in the child's temperament and moods, even though these can be emotionally draining and tiring at times. It is important to remember that children have to learn about and experience a range of positive and negative emotions during infancy and early childhood to develop emotionally.

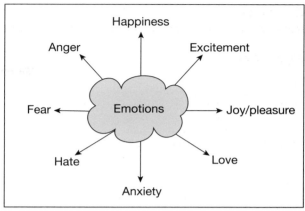

Figure 5.10 Positive and negative emotions

Activity

1. Identify how the following games and activities can be used to encourage and support emotional development during early childhood:
   - peek-a-boo
   - bath time splashing
   - nursery rhymes.
2. Suggest a game or activity that could be used to promote the emotional development of:
   - a 3-month-old baby
   - a 12-month-old infant
   - a 2½-year-old child.

Topic check

1 What does the term 'bonding' mean?
2 Explain why bonding between a baby and parent is thought to be important for emotional development.
3 What does the term 'separation anxiety' mean and when does this occur?
4 Outline four things a parent can do to promote their child's emotional development.
5 Explain what emotional 'regression' involves and identify two reasons why young children sometimes experience this.
6 Summarise the main ways a child develops emotionally between 1 and 3 years of age.

Topic 5.4
Social development and behaviour

 Getting started

This topic focuses on the conditions needed for social development during childhood and on how children can be helped to develop and control their behaviour. When you have completed this topic you should:

- know about factors that influence social development during early childhood
- be able to identify key milestones in social development during early childhood
- understand the links between social development, parental discipline and children's behaviour.

Key terms

Communication skills: language (talking, listening) skills

Discipline: a system of rules that affect an individual's behaviour and self-control

Egocentric: a self-centred person who doesn't take others into account

Punishment: some form of penalty imposed for unacceptable behaviour

Socialisation: the process of learning the behaviours, attitudes, values and way of life of a society

What is social development?

A child's social development affects the relationships they create with others, the social skills they develop and how they learn the culture (or way of life) of society. Parents, carers and teachers have a key role in a child's early social development. During early childhood, parents, teachers and carers teach us:

- ▶ the acceptable ways of behaving
- ▶ how to relate to others in everyday situations
- ▶ the importance of making and keeping good relationships with others.

This process of helping a child to develop socially is known as **socialisation**. A child's early socialisation occurs mainly within their family. At first, a child's parents have the key role to play. However, children gradually expand their social circle during infancy by making relationships with brothers, sisters, other relatives and perhaps neighbours' children. These relationships are strongly influenced by the development of **communication skills**. As they grow and develop intellectually, a child is able to look at the world from the point of view of other people. Children become less **egocentric** as they progress through infancy and early childhood. This is demonstrated by the gradual changes that occur in the way in which children in this age group play (see Topic 5.5).

 Over to you!

Can you remember how your own parents socialised you? Think about what you were taught about 'manners', 'friendships' and 'good behaviour', for example. How would you go about socialising your own child in these areas?

Promoting social development

A parent can promote the social development of their children by:

- creating and maintaining secure, loving relationships with them
- providing their children with lots of play opportunities
- introducing them to other people and the wider social world (e.g. via trips and other interesting activities)
- establishing clear behaviour boundaries and enforcing them firmly and fairly
- encouraging and rewarding their child to share and co-operate with other children
- communicating with them whenever there is an opportunity (e.g. at meal, play and bath times)
- rewarding and reinforcing desirable social attributes and behaviour (e.g. politeness, good manners – saying 'Please' and 'Thank You', blowing their nose appropriately and covering their mouth when coughing, hand washing and sharing)

A child's social development should lead to them feeling good about themselves (self-esteem) and gradually improving their confidence and ability to play, communicate and form relationships independently of their parents. By the age of three, children often want to be more independent, trying things for themselves while being supported by their parents or other adults.

Activity

Children have to learn to share and tolerate others. Parents have an important role to play in teaching their children the importance sharing with others. If you had a 2½-year-old child of your own, or were looking after a child of this age, how could you teach them the importance of sharing? Outline a game, activity or strategy that could be used to socialise a child of this age into sharing with others.

Stages of social development

Children progress through a number of stages of social development and reach developmental milestones ('norms') at approximately the same age. Figure 5.11 describes examples of these milestones.

Children's social development is based on them learning a range of skills. Parents, carers and teachers have to teach, support and provide a range of social learning opportunities for young children so that these skills can be developed. Meeting other children and adults, going to playgroups and nurseries and to the playground to play with other children, as well as interactions in day to day life, provide children with the kinds of social opportunities they need to develop and improve their social skills. Successful social relationships among children are helped by:

- secure attachment in their early years
- mixing with other children, especially where this involves activities that require co-operation
- the personality of the child – friendly, supportive and optimistic children make friends more easily than children who are negative and aggressive.

Figure 5.11 Social development milestones

Age	Development milestone
Birth	A baby will cry when they feel lonely and can be comforted by being cuddled and gently rocked.
1 month	A baby can recognise their mother's face and responds to communication from familiar adults using sounds, eye contact and body language.
3 months	Babies now enjoy company, smile a lot to get attention, communicate pleasure and happiness, and generally enjoy events like feeding and bath time.
6 months	An infant will offers toys to others and will become shy and anxious in the company of strangers.
9 months	An infant will now notice and smile at their own reflection, can join in and enjoy peek-a-boo games and has much greater ability to respond to others.
12 months	An infant will enjoy hugging people they know well and will join in social activities.
15 months	Infants are now becoming more physically capable, more self-confident and will learn to mimic the behaviours, sounds and mannerisms made by others.
18 months	An infant may now appear to be much more sociable with other family members and may approach and socialise with others in a more independent way.
2 years	Children are independent and confident some of the time but insecure and clingy at other times. Children usually know their own name and can refer to themselves using it.
2½ years	A child is able to play alongside other children (parallel play) comfortably, can go to the toilet with help and is able to develop better feeding skills (using a spoon, for example).
3 years	Children can learn to dress and feed themselves with minimal help from parents, like to take part in and help with adult activities and are now able to play more directly with other children (joining-in play).
4 years	A child will now be much more sociable, have a range of basic social skills that allow them to play with other children (co-operative play) and may have learnt to wash and dress themselves with encouragement but minimal help.
5 years	Children are now likely to choose their own friends, are capable of eating using cutlery and in other socially acceptable ways, develop awareness of the needs of others (comforting others when upset or hurt), and know their own name and address.

Negative behaviour and discipline

Learning how to behave in socially acceptable ways is part of both social and emotional development for children. A child may behave in a number of negative ways during early childhood. For example, a child may have temper tantrums, lie, be aggressive, throw toys or other objects, hit, bite, spit or behave badly to get attention.

Negative behaviour in childhood sometimes results from the difficulties children have controlling their emotions. Younger children can also become frustrated by their lack of communication skills and their physical inability to achieve what they want. This is most likely to occur between 2 and 3 years of age when temper tantrums are at their peak. Lying is also quite common at this age, partly because young children find it difficult to distinguish between the 'pretend' play-related aspects of their lives and real life itself. Young children may also not understand the consequences of their behaviour and may not see a 'lie' as a bad thing – particularly if the untruth is more likely to please their mum, dad or teacher than the truth! Despite this, all children need to have the difference between truth and lies, and the importance of not telling lies, explained to them.

Teaching and applying discipline

Parents, carers and teachers have a key role in teaching and applying **discipline**. That is, adults should:

▶ demonstrate a good example through the way they behave and talk to their children

▶ be consistent in the way they approach issues like telling the truth and how they deal with negative behaviour

▶ give children immediate and clear praise for the positive aspects of their behaviour

▶ avoid getting into a 'battle of wills' over behaviour issues with their children

▶ try to divert a child's attention into positive behaviour when they start to slip into negative behaviours.

Parents, carers and teachers need to be fair, firm and consistent in how they manage and respond to a child's behaviour. Good, clear discipline helps a child to:

▶ learn self-control

▶ learn acceptable social behaviour

▶ feel secure and safe because they know where their relationship and behaviour boundaries are.

Praise or punishment?

Discipline for children should be a balanced mix of praise and **punishment**. Rewards are needed to promote positive behaviour. This doesn't mean giving children lots of presents, sweets or food for behaving well! In fact, verbal and social rewards, such as saying 'well done', 'that's great' or 'you're a clever girl', are most effective. When children learn to associate good behaviour with being given food or presents, their good behaviour may come to depend on getting these things rather than on receiving the positive approval of others.

A child's negative behaviour should not be rewarded. At the same time it is important not to punish a child who doesn't understand that their behaviour is 'bad' or unacceptable. Parents should respond to negative behaviour quickly and consistently. It is important to carry out any threatened sanctions ('I'll take that off you') or verbal warnings will become ineffective. Smacking children for negative behaviour is a very controversial practice. Smacking does not teach a child how to behave and runs the risk of making aggression and hitting others seem like acceptable behaviour. More appropriate types of punishment include:

▶ disapproval of the behaviour and withdrawal of attention

▶ explaining why the child can't have or do something

▶ removing objects, stopping activities or taking the child away from problem situations.

 Over to you!

How many different phrases can you think of that could be used to praise a child for positive behaviour? Make a list of these and compare them with a colleague's list.

Figure 5.12 Examples of responses to negative behaviour

Type of behaviour	Possible response
Aggression – e.g. kicking, biting, shouting, hitting, throwing, spitting	• Stop the child from hurting others or themselves. • Disapprove of the behaviour without rejecting the child. • Withdraw attention. • Explain why this behaviour is not acceptable.
Attention-seeking behaviour – e.g. efforts to obtain parent's attention through negative behaviours such as screaming, holding breath or refusing food	• 'Extinguish' the behaviour by ignoring it (ensuring child is safe) – it will decline if it is unrewarded. • Give child time and attention when behaving appropriately. • Talk to child in positive ways, building up self-esteem, confidence and sense of security.

Activity

Lana, aged 3, has recently started throwing wooden building blocks and lego bricks around here bedroom whenever her mum gets them out for her to play with. She used to really enjoy playing quietly with them. Initially, Lana's mum asked her not to throw toys around her room and told her that she might accidently break the mirror or a window. Lana said she understood that she shouldn't do this. However, earlier this week, Lana did throw some wooden building blocks around her room. One of them hit and broke the bedroom window. Despite being the only person in the room, Lana denied (and still won't admit) throwing the blocks. This has left her mum feeling exasperated and angry with her.

1. Make a list of reasons why Lana might have taken to throwing her wooden building blocks.

2. Has Lana's mum done all she can, or are there other things she could do to prevent Lana from carrying on with this behaviour?

3. Should Lana's mum expect her to always tell the truth and admit when she has been naughty or done something wrong?

Parents need to achieve a consistent and balanced approach to disciplining their children because too much or too little discipline can be problematic for a child's development. For example, too much discipline can:

▶ cause a child to feel negative and self-critical

▶ put too many expectations and too much pressure on a child

▶ damage the parent–child relationship if either loses trust in or respect for the other.

A parent who over-disciplines their children can become overly critical and non-nurturing. As a result, their children may develop a negative self-concept and grow up believing they are unable to please people or do anything right. Too little, inconsistent or unclear discipline, on the other hand, can:

▶ cause a child to feel insecure

▶ result in a child becoming rude, aggressive and selfish towards others

▶ encourage disobedience and lack of respect towards others.

A child who lacks discipline may grow up to be inconsiderate and may be seen to be selfish and badly behaved by others.

Discipline is a difficult issue for many parents who may or may not agree on the best approach to take. It has to be introduced gradually, because a child must understand the reasons for discipline and behaviour 'rules' in order to comply with them. Children can understand what 'no' means as early as 1 year old. However, they don't really understand why they should behave in some ways rather than others or what 'lying' means until much later in childhood. As children grow and develop greater understanding, they become more aware of the expectations and boundaries that apply to their behaviour.

Activity

Imagine that a friend or relative who has a 2-year-old child asks you what she can do to teach her child 'good behaviour'. Produce a list of guidelines to help her based on what you have learnt about social development, behaviour and discipline in this topic.

Topic check

1 What does the term 'socialisation' mean?

2 Describe three ways in which parents can promote their children's social development.

3 Describe the kinds of social skills children develop in the first 18 months of life.

4 Outline three of the factors that contribute to effective social development during early childhood.

5 Describe two examples of negative social behaviours that children sometimes develop in early childhood.

6 Explain how parents can respond to their children's negative social behaviour in early childhood, indicating the advantages and disadvantages of two different approaches.

Play

▶ Getting started

This topic focuses on different types of play and how children develop and learn through play. When you have completed this topic you should:

■ be able to identify and describe different types of play

■ know how children's play changes as they grow and develop in early childhood

■ understand the importance of choosing safe and age appropriate toys for younger children.

Key terms

Crèche: a day nursery for pre-school age children and infants, often located in a workplace or shopping centre

Exploratory: based on discovering or investigating

Hazardous: something that presents a risk or danger

Kindergarten: a pre-school service for children aged 4 to 6 years, usually to prepare them for starting school

Risk assessment: the process of examining whether a toy or other object may injure or harm a child

Solitary: doing something alone

Play and social learning

Children who attend pre-school childcare and early years learning settings such as playgroups, nurseries, **crèches**, **kindergartens** and childminders, participate in lots of play activities. This is because play provides a wide range of learning opportunities for pre-school children. Learning to play with other children by sharing toys, taking turns and co-operating provides some early social development opportunities, for example. A child's social skills develop and improve as they learn to communicate and spend time with other children taking part in different types of play activity.

Solitary or solo play

The first stage of play involves a child playing alone. Babies and young children can be very contented playing on their own and frequently show no interest in wanting to play with others. This gradually changes as the child becomes more aware of and able to communicate with other children.

Parallel play

This type of play involves a child playing alongside – but not with – another child. Children move from **solitary**/solo play to parallel play as they build up their self-confidence and become more familiar with other children.

Looking-on play

This involves a child watching other children playing, often from the edge of a group of children or across a playground. The child shows interest in the activities of other children by looking-on but isn't ready or confident enough to join in.

Joining-in play

This occurs where a child is motivated and confident enough to join in play activities with another child. They may not be deliberately co-operating or sharing but will be happy to participate in the same type of play activity.

Co-operative play

This is the stage of play where children actually co-operate with each other, playing together in a deliberate way. Co-operative play can occur between a couple of children who communicate and share an activity together or within a larger group of children.

Learning through play

Play is a natural, enjoyable way for children to learn. Children can use play to investigate and explore the world around them, develop their physical, intellectual and social skills and as a way of expressing their imagination and emotions.

Physical play

Children can use lots of different physical play activities, such as jumping, riding scooters and bicycles, running and playing with balls, trampolines and climbing equipment, to develop their gross and fine motor skills. Physical play is a way of getting and keeping a child's developing body in good shape, and provides children with an outlet for their physical energy and ways of testing out the physical skills and abilities they develop.

Creative play

Painting, colouring, making music, using construction toys and cooking are all play activities that allow a child to develop and use their creativity. Creative play enables a child to develop and use intellectual and physical – especially fine motor – skills as it usually involves activities that are both mentally absorbing and 'hands on'.

Imaginative play

'Let's pretend' games and other imaginative play activities become a feature of children's play from about the age of 2. Children have more language ability and can use this and their developing knowledge of the world to make up games or role-play what they see around them. Dressing up tends to be a very popular activity with both boys and girls during this stage of early childhood.

Role-play games in which children pretend to be 'mum', 'dad', their teacher or another significant adult, acting out stories or pretending to be characters from their favourite cartoons are ways children explore, develop and express emotions in a safe, non-threatening way.

Exploratory play

This type of play involves children exploring the use of their senses to learn about the world around them. Babies do a lot of this when they touch, hold and squeeze objects. As they become more mobile and curious, babies will also suck and smell objects and the things they can reach as a way of finding out about them. Young children are often attracted to shiny, glittery and noisy toys and objects that make them curious. Playing exploratory games with objects that have a strong sensory appeal is a way of finding out about their properties and of learning about ideas like weight, shape, colour and texture.

Manipulative play

Hand and eye coordination can be developed through manipulative play activities. This might include using rattles, putting simple jigsaw pieces together, playing with dolls houses, pushing buttons and levers on activity centre toys or putting differently shaped wooden blocks and pegs into appropriately shaped holes. Children learn how to handle and manipulate different types of materials and how to solve simple problems through this type of play.

Social play

Social play involves co-operation with other children (and sometimes adults). It enables children to learn how to tolerate others, and to share and work with them. Children can learn to understand the roles, needs and perspectives of others through social play. Playing closely and co-operatively with other children also requires the child to control their own behaviour and express their emotions in a socially acceptable way.

When you observe children playing, you will probably realise a number of these types of play occur during a play activity. This is because they are all linked. Playing a 'let's pretend' game about 'hiding from the dragon' may involve imaginative, physical and social play, for example. Similarly, making some simple cakes can involve creative, **exploratory** and manipulative play. The key points to remember about play are that it:

▶ provides learning opportunities for children

▶ engages children in stimulating and constructive activity

▶ enables children to develop a positive sense of achievement and wellbeing.

Activity

Imagine that you are a playgroup assistant. You have been asked to identify three different games or activities for next week's session. These should be suitable for children aged 2–3 years of age and should enable the children to use:

• physical and manipulative skills
• creativity and imagination
• social and exploratory skills.

Wendy, aged three, like to play 'supermarkets' with her twin brother Brandon. This involves Wendy loading plastic fruit and other toys into her toy pram. She also puts 'Lawrence the lion' her favourite cuddly toy in the pram. Wendy and Lawrence then go over to the sofa, where Brandon is standing. He takes the fruit from her and says 'bip' as he puts each piece into a basket. When he has 'bipped' all of the fruit, he announces the price ('That's ten pounds, please'). Wendy then pretends to pay, says

'Thank you' and wheels the fruit and Lawrence away. Finally she announces 'I've been to the supermarket'.

1. What kinds of play are involved in the 'supermarket' game?

2. What sort of skills is Brandon developing and using in this game?

3. How does the 'supermarket' game help Wendy to develop her social skills?

Choosing and using toys

There is now a huge range of toys available for babies and children of all ages. Despite this, babies and children are often as interested in the box or packaging toys come in, and sometimes treat household objects as toys to play with too! Babies and children like toys to play and need them to promote their development. Regardless of whether they have been specially designed and produced for play purposes or as other household objects, the toys a child plays with should always be:

▶ stimulating and enjoyable

▶ safe and non-hazardous

▶ suitable for the child's age and stage of development

▶ appealing to the child

▶ durable.

Safety issues

Health and safety issues are sometimes seen as 'anti-fun' and as something that parents and childcare workers shouldn't be too concerned about. However, toys that are badly made or that are constructed from potentially **hazardous** materials may have a direct and long-lasting impact on a child's health. All toys given to babies and children in the UK should meet minimum safety standards. Those that do will have safety symbols printed on their labels or on the toys themselves (see Figure 5.13).

When you are choosing toys for a child, you should check for:

▶ sharp edges, staples, pins or spikes that might injure a child

▶ loose or ill-fitting parts that can be removed and swallowed

▶ lead-free paint and non-toxic glues

▶ the CE 'lion' mark indicating a safe toy

▶ durability (will the toy stand rough treatment?).

It is important to carry out a **risk assessment** on every toy in order to identify any potential hazards it might contain or problems that might occur in the way a particular child uses it.

Figure 5.13 Safety symbols for toys

Figure 5.14 Developmentally appropriate toys

Age	Abilities	Suitable toys
Birth to 6 months	Listening, looking, reaching and grasping	Rattles, mobiles, soft toys, teddies, plastic rings and keys, musical toys
6–12 months	Holding and basic manipulation of objects, better hand-eye coordination, sitting and crawling	Push and pull along toys, basic construction toys, activity centre with lots of buttons and sounds, stacking beakers
12–18 months	Basic balance and walking skills improving, more effective hand–eye coordination, developing language skills	Shape sorters, pop-up, picture and 'lift the flap' books, sand and water, mini trampoline
18 months to 2 years	Running, climbing, improved strength, stamina and hand–eye coordination	Simple jigsaws, balls, short story books, nursery rhyme books, play house or 'tent'
2–3 years	Improving fine motor skills, ability to recognise colours, sizes, can sit still and listen	Picture books, paint and paper, dominoes and cards to match up, pedal car or tricycle, toy pram to push
3–4 years	Good gross motor skills, better strength, improving balance, basic numeracy concepts, developing imagination	Scooter, bicycle, swing, dressing up clothes and hats, construction toys, puppets and dolls, toy cars
4–5 years	Good concentration and hand-eye coordination, improving language and basic numeracy skills, good balance and fine motor control, good imagination	Number-based games (clocks, shop tills, weighing scales), alphabet games and jigsaws, 'let's pretend' kitchen utensils and gardening equipment

The way a child uses a toy is likely to depend on their stage of development. Many children find new uses for their 'old' toys as they grow and develop. Rather than continually replacing toys with new, apparently more age-specific toys, it is often a good idea to let a child use their imagination and the knowledge and skills they have gained through development to continue to enjoy and benefit from some of their favourite toys. A child may find interesting and beneficial uses of an 'old' toy as their physical, intellectual, emotional, social and language skills develop and enable them to do new things with it.

 Activity

Using catalogues (printed or on the Internet), choose a developmentally appropriate toy or game to give to each of the following children:

- Dexter will soon be 4 years of age. He has good imagination and like building things.
- Lily will be 1 year old next month. She is just starting to walk.
- Ben is 2 years of age on Saturday. He likes stories and using his boundless energy.

Write a short explanation of the reasons why you chose each toy.

 Topic check

1 Identify five different types of play.
2 Describe how a child can develop through physical play.
3 Explain the benefits of social play for a child's development.
4 What should you always check for when choosing toys for a child?
5 Explain why toys should be 'developmentally appropriate' for children.
6 At approximately what age would it be appropriate for a child to have a bicycle (without stabilisers)? Explain your answer by referring to the skills and abilities a child needs to ride a bicycle.

6 Community support

Introduction

This chapter is divided into four topics:

6.1 Day care provision and pre-school learning

6.2 Statutory services for children and families

6.3 Private and voluntary services for children and families

6.4 Children with special needs

Overall, this chapter introduces you to a range of topics and issues relating to the services and forms of support provided for children and families. Topic 6.1 describes different types of day care services and explains the purpose of the Early Years Foundation Stage of learning. Topic 6.2 outlines different forms of statutory provision for children and families and explains how to gain access to these services. Topic 6.3 describes the role and provision of private and voluntary sector services for children and families, and explains how these can be obtained. Topic 6.4 describes and explains the reasons why some children have special needs. You will also learn about ways of caring for babies and young children with special needs.

By the end of this chapter you should be able to recognise and understand:

▶ that there are a range of different forms of day care for pre-school children in the UK

▶ that there are a range of statutory services for children and families that can be accessed through referral

▶ that private and voluntary sector organisations and practitioners provide a range of services for children and families throughout the UK

▶ that some children have special needs that require additional and specialist forms of care and support.

Day care provision and pre-school learning

Getting started

This topic focuses on day care provision for pre-school age children. When you have completed this topic you should:

- understand why families use day care provision for their children
- be able to identify a range of types of day care provision for pre-school children
- know about the Early Years Foundation Stage (EYFS) of learning.

Key terms

Childcare swaps: this happens when parents take it in turns to look after each other's children on an informal basis

EYFS: an acronym for Early Years Foundation Stage

OFSTED: an acronym for the Office for Standards in Education

Phonic knowledge: learning that involves associating letters with their sounds

Regulated: governed or controlled

Special needs: the additional or further needs for assistance people have because of an illness or disability

Day care provision in the UK

Day care is the term given to forms of childcare provided during the day by someone who is not the child's parent or legal guardian. Day care providers look after and supervise children during periods when their parents can't do this.

The need and demand for day care provision for pre-school children has grown steadily over the last 25 years throughout the UK. There are a number of reasons for this including:

▶ The number of women working either full or part-time during the day has increased. In 2002, 52 per cent of women with a child under 5 years old and 70 per cent of women with a child 5–10 years of age were working either full or part-time.

▶ It has been recognised that children's development benefits from pre-school play and early education opportunities.

▶ The number and type of pre-school day care providers has grown.

▶ Childcare funding from employers and government sources has increased.

▶ Provision of day care services for children with **special needs** has grown.

A large number of parents now use day care services, informal family support (particularly grandparents) and **childcare swaps** to obtain day care for their children while they work or attend educational courses.

Figure 6.1 Pre-school attendance of 3 and 4 year olds by type of early years provider (January 2003)

Country	Three and four year olds in early years education (thousands)	Maintained nursery and primary schools	Independent and special schools	All schools	Private and voluntary providers	All providers
England	1,190.6	59	5	64	38	102
Wales	55.6	78	1	79	0	79
Scotland	100.7	–	–	65	26	91
N. Ireland	32.9	58	1	59	13	71

Source: Department for Education and Skills; National Assembly for Wales; Scottish Executive; Northern Ireland Department of Education

Employers increasingly offer flexible working arrangements to enable parents to combine their work and childcare responsibilities. Following a change in the law, parents can now request flexible working arrangements such as the following:

▶ Job sharing – where two people share one job. Job share partners divide the hours required to perform their work and make arrangements between themselves about how to cover the hours. Both job share partners earn a share of the salary, with the amount dependent on what proportion of the required hours they work. Most people choose to job share because they wish to work but also want to have time with their own children.

▶ Flexible hours – where an individual fits work around childcare responsibilities. This is often done by starting and finishing each working day at times that are convenient for childcare (e.g. early start/early finish).

▶ Working from home – where an individual carries out their job from their own home. This tends to rely on the person being able to use information and computer technologies and having a job that doesn't require them to be located in a particular place. Some people work from home for part of their working week to enable them to fit work around childcare responsibilities. Other people spend the whole of their week working from home.

Pre-school learning

Children's learning during the pre-school phase is **regulated** by the **EYFS** curriculum. This sets out the child welfare, and learning and development standards and requirements that must be met by providers of care for children under 5. Since September 2008, all day care providers, including childminders, nurseries and pre-school classes, have had to implement the EYFS. The EYFS has caused some controversy because it imposes compulsory literacy and numeracy targets for children under 5. For example, pre-school children are expected to:

▶ use written language in their play and learning

▶ use **phonic knowledge** to write simple words

▶ be able to find information in non-fiction books to answer questions about where, who, why and how

▶ begin to form simple sentences, sometimes using punctuation.

Some day care providers have criticised the requirements of the EYFS saying that it:

▶ pushes children into learning literacy and numeracy too early

▶ prevents children from enjoying and experimenting with learning through play

▶ imposes stressful demands on very young children

▶ causes some children ongoing reading problems because they have an early experience of failure.

People who argue in favour of the EYFS say that it:

▶ establishes clear, national standards for learning and development in the pre-school years

▶ ensures that all children have equal opportunities to develop their knowledge and learning skills before they start school

▶ provides a way of monitoring the performance of early years providers

▶ improves opportunities and raises standards for pre-school children.

All providers of pre-school childcare and early years services now have to be registered and are inspected by **OFSTED** to ensure they are meeting the learning and development requirements of the EYFS.

Over to you!

What do you think about the EYFS curriculum? If you had a 3-year-old child, would you want them to begin learning about reading and writing at pre-school nursery? Or do you think they should be allowed to use their pre-school time to just play?

Types of day care provision

There are a number of different types of day care service in the UK. All day care providers have to be registered and must follow government guidelines on staffing, facilities and safety.

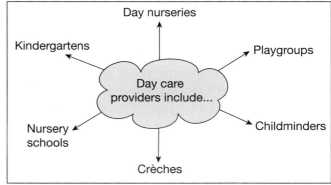

Figure 6.2 Types of day care provider

Day nurseries

Day nurseries offer a range of childcare and early education services. They are aimed at children under 5 who attend while their parents are at work. Some day nurseries are run by local authorities though the majority are provided by private and voluntary sector organisations. People use this form of day care provision because they:

▶ operate at times that suit working parents

▶ provide services that are closely regulated and monitored by OFSTED and others

▶ give children opportunities to develop social skills and relationships with other children in a structured environment

▶ provide a range of age-appropriate resources, activities and learning opportunities for pre-school children.

Workplace crèches

Workplace crèches are a type of nursery that cater for the children of parents in a particular workplace. The crèche is usually provided or funded by the parent's employer and is typically on the same site as the parent's workplace. A workplace crèche will provide the same kinds of early years service and care as a day nursery.

Nursery schools

Nursery schools, also known as pre-schools, offer children a more formal educational experience and environment than day nurseries. The activities that are provided for children are still often delivered through play and creative activity but tend to have an explicit learning focus. There has been a significant increase in the numbers of children attending nursery schools as a result of changes to government policy and funding over the last 10 years. Every child is entitled to free nursery school provision, beginning in the first term after their third birthday. Many nursery schools are provided and run by local authorities, though there are also a lot of private and voluntary sector providers throughout the UK. Like day nurseries, pre-school nurseries are monitored and inspected by OFSTED and must meet the requirements of the EYFS.

Activity

Where are the pre-school nurseries in your local area? Carry out some research to try and identify the location and admission criteria of a range of day nurseries, nurseries and pre-school playgroups within a 5-mile radius of your home or school/college. Produce a table summarising your findings, ideally with a map showing the location (and type) of pre-school provision available to children and families in your area.

Childminders

Childminders provide care for other people's pre-school children in the childminder's home environment. Childminders care for much smaller groups of children than nursery schools or day nurseries. The group of children being cared for may include one or more of a childminder's own children. All childminders now have to be registered with their local authority, must implement the EYFS curriculum and are inspected by OFSTED to ensure that the care and early education provision they offer meets the required standard.

Parents may choose to use a childminder because:

▶ childminders offer hours that are very flexible – perhaps starting earlier and finishing later than other types of service provider

▶ some parents prefer a more homely environment for their children, seeing this as less threatening than a school or day care nursery environment – this can be an important consideration when the child is very young

▶ a childminder may charge lower fees than day nurseries

▶ childminder services provide children with opportunities to socialise with and get to know other children in a smaller, more supportive group and in a family environment.

Playgroups

Playgroups are usually provided on a voluntary basis, often in community centres, church halls or other public venues. Many playgroups only run in term time as they are often staffed by parent volunteers. The age range of children attending playgroups varies but, in general, playgroups cater for 'toddlers' (2–4 year olds). The manager or leader of a playgroup often has childcare or infant teaching qualifications and experience. The number of children attending playgroups has declined significantly over the last 10 years. There are a number of reasons for this, including:

▶ a growth in the numbers of women working who need full-time day care and who are unable to take their children to a playgroup themselves

▶ a growth in the number of nursery schools providing pre-school education and play opportunities for children from 3 years of age.

The main characteristic of playgroups is the way they use play as an early education tool. Sessions are organised around different forms of play that are designed to have informal learning benefits for young children.

Topic check

1 Identify three forms of day care provision available for young children in the UK.
2 Describe two forms of flexible working arrangements parents sometimes use to cope with their combined childcare and work.
3 What is the EYFS and how does it affect day care provision for pre-school children?
4 What role does OFSTED play in day care provision for pre-school children?
5 Outline three reasons why parents sometimes employ childminders to look after their pre-school children.
6 Describe the main characteristics of playgroups for pre-school children.

Statutory services for children and families

Getting started

This topic focuses on the range of statutory (government) services and forms of support that are provided for children and families. When you have completed this topic you should:

■ be able to identify the main sources and forms of statutory services for children and families

■ know about different forms of financial support that are available from statutory services

■ understand how families can access statutory services and support for their children.

Key terms

Local authorities: government organisations responsible for the local provision of early years, social care and education services

Means-test: a test that determines whether an individual or family is eligible to qualify for help or a service

Multi-agency working: this involves a team of health, early years and social care workers who are

employed by different agencies (care organisations) working together as part of the same team to provide care for a particular individual or group of people

NHS: an acronym for the National Health Service

Partnership working: typically this involves different organisations working together (as partners) to provide a service

Statutory: relating to the law (statute)

Services for children and families

Most of the health and educational needs of children and families throughout the UK are met by **statutory** providers of care services, such as **local authorities** (councils) and the **NHS**. In addition to this, a range of voluntary and private sector organisations and practitioners exist throughout the UK and are the source of many of the childcare, social support and early education services that are used by children and families.

By law, government organisations such as the NHS and local authorities have to provide some types of care and welfare services for families and individuals in a local community. They also provide services that benefit all members of the local community and maintain the local environment. These services include:

▶ housing, education and health services for children and families

▶ facilities, such as parks, sports centres and libraries, that provide development opportunities

▶ community safety and emergency services (fire, police, ambulance, accident and emergency, etc.) that safeguard and protect children and families

▶ street cleaning, refuse collection and recycling services that ensure the local environment is safe and clean for children and families.

Statutory support for families

Every local authority in the UK has a responsibility to provide services that meet the needs of children and families. Local authorities usually have specialist children and families and education departments that provide and monitor early years, social work and family support services for children and families who are in need or 'at risk'. In addition, local NHS primary care services and NHS Trust hospitals provide a range of statutory health-related services for all children and families.

Statutory services for children and families are obtained through a referral system. The different types of referral that exist include:

▶ self-referral (by a parent or carer)

▶ professional referral (by a GP, health visitor or teacher, for example)

▶ third-party referral (by a relative or friend).

 Over to you!

Do you know what your local authority is called and where it is located? Try to find this out and also obtain information on the kinds of services for children that are offered by your local NHS primary care service and NHS Trust hospital.

 Case study

Helen, aged 22, is a lone parent. She has a 1-year-old daughter called Emma. Helen suffered from postnatal depression for several months after Emma was born. Initially she just thought that she was tired and couldn't cope with the stress of looking after Emma on her own. Helen's health visitor provided her with a lot of support and encouraged her to go and see her GP. Helen's GP diagnosed postnatal depression and referred her to the Children's Centre for support and to a Young Mum's group that was run at a local authority day centre. Helen is very grateful for the help and support she gets at the Children's Centre. She now takes Emma there three times a week. She also attends the Young Mum's group every fortnight.

This is run by Janice, a social worker, but is very informal. She has made a number of friends who are in a similar position and often meets them at their homes or in the park. Helen had to have her needs assessed before she was able to use the two services. However, she passed both a means-test and other eligibility criteria because she is on a low income and has little home support.

1. Which two statutory sector services provide support for Helen and Emma?

2. How did Helen gain access to these two services?

3. Explain what a means-test is and the reason Helen passed this.

Social work and child protection services

Local authorities employ both general social workers and specialist child protection social workers to provide support and assistance to children and families. Typically a social worker will visit and support children and families at home with the aim of keeping them together, living in their own home. Local authority social workers usually work with families who have been referred to them because they are 'in need' of support or services or because they are 'at risk' in some way. To provide the kinds of help or assistance a family requires, a social worker will first assess the needs of individual family members and the family as a whole. Following this they may:

▶ refer the family to relevant specialist services (housing, debt counselling, benefits agency) for specific support or assistance

▶ act as an advocate for the family (representing and speaking on behalf of the family to get their views across in court or at case conferences, for example)

▶ carry out 'risk assessments' and monitor child welfare if child protection issues are a feature of the family's problems or difficulties.

A family may require support and assistance from local authority statutory services for a short period of time until their problems are resolved. Other families may require ongoing and more complex forms of support and assistance because their problems and needs are more involved. The forms of support provided by the statutory (government) system for children and families tend to be a response to the particular needs of a family. For example, some families have housing needs whereas others may have welfare benefits, educational or childcare needs. In some cases, a family may have a combination of these needs and will receive a more complex package of support and assistance.

Needs of low-income and lone-parent families

Families tend to be in greatest need when their children are young, when both parents are unemployed or on a low income, or when a lone parent has to try and meet the needs of themselves and their children. Local authorities often assess the needs of low-income and lone-parent families, and provide assistance and referral to appropriate resources (see Figure 6.3).

In many cases, financial support from the benefits system enables low income and lone-parent families to meet their everyday living needs.

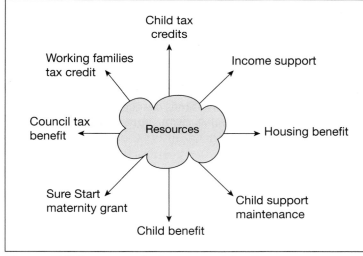

Figure 6.3 Resources for lone-parent families

Financial support for families

Families can now claim a range of benefits and tax credits. Advice on these is available online from organisations such as the Citizens Advice Bureau (CAB) (www.adviceguide.org.uk), the Inland Revenue (HMRC) (www.hmrc.gov.uk/childbenefit) or from local benefits agency offices.

Most welfare benefits for families are means-tested. That is, a family's income is assessed and compared against a scale for working out benefits. The principle of means-testing ensures that people who have more income receive fewer welfare benefits, and vice versa. This enables the government to target means-tested benefits at those most in need.

Examples of means-tested benefits currently available to families with children include:

▶ Working tax credit – this supports people who are working part-time or who are unemployed, to ensure they have a minimum amount of income.

▶ Housing benefit/council tax benefits – these benefits provide assistance with the cost of housing for low income families.

▶ Sure Start grants – these are single payments for low income families that are designed to help them pay for the costs of a new baby.

Tax credits

The tax credits system is a relatively new way of paying welfare benefits. Tax credits are payments from the government to families and young people who are living on low incomes. They aim to help people afford the day to day costs of living. Different forms of tax credits exist, including:

▶ Child tax credit – this is paid mainly to families with children under 16 years of age (but up to 20 in some cases). These are direct payments made to the person responsible for the children in a family. Child tax credits can consist of family, child and disability elements.

▶ Working tax credit – this is paid to working parents (16+ hours/week) and disabled people who are aged 25+ and working more than 30 hours per week.

The amounts people are entitled to claim through the tax credits system change each year and there are sometimes changes to the eligibility criteria. Details of current tax credit rates and eligibility criteria can be obtained by visiting the CAB or HMRC websites, or a local benefits agency office.

Over to you!

Why do you think some people are reluctant to undergo **means-tests** and fail to collect benefits they could otherwise obtain? Make a list of possible reasons and share ideas with a class colleague.

Universal benefits

Though most welfare benefits are means-tested, there are also some universal benefits that are automatically available to everybody who meets the eligibility criteria, regardless of their income. Examples include:

▶ child benefit – an allowance paid by government to parents for each of their children until the child leaves education or is 18 years of age

▶ disability living allowance – an allowance paid by government to cover the cost of caring for a disabled child or adult who has care needs or mobility problems

▶ free dental treatment and prescription charges – available for all children until they leave full-time education, and for pregnant women and mothers with children under 1 year of age who have a valid exemption certificate.

Other types of benefit

A number of other types of benefit are also available to working parents to help them at times when they have significant childcare needs. These include:

▶ statutory maternity pay – a payment made by the government to women who have worked for the same employer for 6 months

▶ maternity allowance – a payment made to women who don't qualify for statutory maternity pay

▶ Health in Pregnancy grant – a one-off grant given to women who are 25 weeks pregnant to help them prepare for the birth of their baby

▶ statutory paternity pay – a payment made by government to working men who take paternity leave following the birth of their child.

Men and women both have the right to take unpaid leave from their employment to look after their children. In these cases, people can be eligible for income support, housing benefit, council tax benefit and tax credit payments.

Unclaimed benefits

Even though a range of benefits are available to families with children, some people don't obtain or take them because:

▶ they don't know about them

▶ they are too difficult to obtain (complex form filling, long, expensive phone calls, long distances to interview appointments)

▶ language barriers prevent them knowing about or obtaining their entitlement

▶ they are embarrassed about claiming benefits because they associate them with 'charity' or 'poverty'.

GPs, health visitors and social workers can often explain, help with and make referrals for welfare benefits. Families who don't claim the benefits they are entitled to are likely to have fewer resources to meet their children's health and development needs. In addition to welfare benefits, a number of government initiatives have been developed to address the needs of children and families who are in need. These include:

▶ integrated children's services
▶ Welfare to Work
▶ Sure Start Children's Centres.

Integrated children's services

Integrated children's services are a new feature of statutory services that have been developed throughout the UK since the Children Act (2004) was passed. This piece of legislation is the result of a government policy called *Every Child Matters*.

The *Every Child Matters* policy put forward the idea of linking together (integrating) all of the services that children come into contact with. The importance of integrating children's services became very clear following the death of Victoria Climbié, an 8-year-old girl, in 2000. Victoria died as a result of severe physical abuse that was caused by her aunt and her aunt's boyfriend who were supposed to be caring for her. Victoria's death occurred despite the fact that care professionals from several different care organisations had come into contact with her. The fact that the different care professionals who had concerns about Victoria didn't communicate with each other or take responsibility for stopping what was happening occurred because of a lack of **multi-agency** and **partnership working**.

Integrated children's services now offer joined-up health, social care and education services to vulnerable children and their families through children's centres, extended schools, youth clubs and health care clinics. A local integrated children's service will typically:

▶ be the first point of contact for all enquiries from children, families and professionals
▶ receive and make referrals for services for children
▶ identify, refer and monitor vulnerable children.

The care practitioners who are employed by an integrated children's service:

▶ assess service users' needs
▶ give information and advice
▶ receive and make referrals for emergency and preventive services
▶ complete and manage information about a child and their family.

 Over to you!

Have you thought about any aspects of child development that you might want to focus on as part of your assessment? Your first step will be to identify a child whom you can observe. Can you think of anyone who might let you observe their child?

Integrating children's services is seen as a way of protecting vulnerable children and of improving the opportunities and life experiences of the poorest and most disadvantaged children. Examples of integrated children's services include:

▶ Sure Start Children's Centres (0–5s) that offer childcare, health and family welfare services

▶ extended schools (primary and secondary) that offer out of hours activities, parenting support, childcare, community health services, adult learning and recreational activities

▶ multi-agency disability teams that provide a single point of referral, assessment and treatment for children and young people with physical, learning or sensory disabilities.

Integrated children's services are a new form of statutory care provision that combines health, social care and early years provision in order to target the needs of vulnerable children and families. As a result, these services break down the traditional organisational barriers between health, social care and early years services.

Activity

Identify the location of your nearest Sure Start Children's Centre. Find out:

- what services are available at the centre
- who the services are provided for
- which health, social care and early years professionals work at the centre
- what the aims and objectives of the centre are
- what the benefits of using the centre are to service users.

Welfare to Work

This is a government initiative designed to support and encourage people on benefits to obtain paid work. Lone parents, for example, are targeted through the Welfare to Work scheme with advice, training and financial child care assistance to enable them to obtain employment. Extended schools provision is also part of the support offered to enable some parents to go to work while also managing childcare responsibilities. The Welfare to Work scheme is designed to help vulnerable and disadvantaged families to improve their quality of life by escaping dependency on welfare benefits. Despite these aims, it has been criticised by some for not taking into account the realities and difficulties of being a working lone parent.

Over to you!

Can you think of any limitations or criticisms of Welfare to Work? Why might lone parents, for example, find it difficult to hold a full-time job and be the main source of childcare for their children?

Sure Start

The Sure Start programme is a government initiative that is designed to give disadvantaged children the best start in life. Sure Start Children's Centres are part of integrated children's services (see above). They provide information and advice on health, early education and support services for children and families. Children's centres that bring together childcare, early education, health and family support services for under 5s are also now available nationally.

Activity

Go to the Department for Children, Schools and families website (http://www.dcsf.gov.uk/everychildmatters/earlyyears/surestart/surestartchild renscentres/childrenscentres/) and select the FAQ (Frequently Asked Questions) and the 'History of Sure Start' pages. Summarise the key points about the purpose of this type of early years care provision and the range of services that are provided through Sure Start.

Topic check

1 Identify the two main sources of statutory services for children and families in the UK.
2 Describe the main ways of obtaining services for children and families from statutory services.
3 Identify three different examples of welfare benefits that are provided to children and families by the government.
4 Why do some people not claim the welfare benefits they are entitled to?
5 What kinds of help and support are available to children and families from integrated children's services?
6 What is the Welfare to Work programme?

Private and voluntary services for children and families

Getting started

This topic focuses on the range of private and voluntary sector services and forms of support that are provided for children and families. When you have completed this topic you should:

- be able to identify the main sources and forms of private and voluntary sector services for children and families
- understand how families can obtain private and voluntary sector services and support for their children.

Key terms

Childminder: a private sector childcare provider who offers day care for a small number of children in the childminder's own home

Independent sector: this term is sometimes used to refer to the private and voluntary sectors that are independent of government

Private sector: this consists of organisations and

self-employed care practitioners who charge a fee for their services

Subsidise: pay part of the cost

Voluntary sector: this consists of large and small organisations that are independent of government and provide services on a not-for-profit basis

Independent sector providers

Voluntary and **private sector** services for children and families are provided by a range of non-governmental organisations, volunteers and self-employed practitioners throughout the UK. Altogether these service providers are sometimes known as the **independent sector** because they generally work independently of government.

Voluntary sector services

The voluntary early years sector consists of:

▶ large national organisations, such as the NSPCC (www.nspcc.org.uk), Barnardo's (www.barnardos.org.uk) and The Children's Society (www.childrenssociety.org.uk)

▶ small, local voluntary groups who provide playgroups, nurseries and other support groups for children under the age of 8 and their parents.

The voluntary early years sector is a major provider of early years services throughout the UK. Small, local voluntary sector groups:

▶ provide forms of support, early education and childcare that are not available elsewhere

▶ offer play opportunities, mutual support, information and practical childcare assistance for parents

▶ are often run by parents whose children who are not eligible for statutory services and who also cannot afford, or don't wish to pay for, private early years care

▶ can often respond flexibly and quickly to the needs of children and families

▶ rely on small donations or voluntary help to fund and run their services.

Larger, national voluntary organisations, such as The Children's Society, Childline and the Family Welfare Association:

▶ work either independently or with local authorities to provide local services

▶ have trained, employed and volunteer staff, often with specific childcare and early years experience

▶ provide direct assistance, campaigning to bring about change, confidential support, counselling, advice and practical help for children and families who have personal, social or financial needs that can't be met by statutory services.

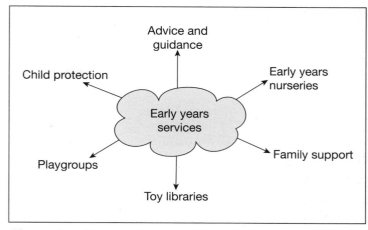

Figure 6.4 Examples of early years services provided by voluntary organisations

 Activity

Use the internet, library or other resources to find out about the range of services for children and families that are offered by:

- The Children's Society
- The Family Welfare Association
- Citizens Advice Bureau
- NSPCC
- TAMBA (Twins and Multiple Births Association)
- Gingerbread.

 Case study

Jill runs a pre-school playgroup between 10 a.m. and 11.30 a.m. on a Monday for children under the age of five. The playgroup use the back room of a church hall which is always provided free of charge. They have a large cupboard full of donated toys and games, an indoor slide and a couple of tricycles. Jill is a volunteer and runs the playgroup on behalf of the Church group who own the hall. A small fee of £1 per child is charged to cover the cost of drinks and snacks for the children and tea and coffee for the parents. Jill organises the group, reads stories and sings songs to the children who attend and tries to ensure that a variety of age-appropriate toys and games are available each morning. She encourages parents to take part but there is no requirement to do so. Many of the parents who come like to spend time chatting with each other while their children play in a safe environment.

1. Is Jill's playgroup an example of voluntary or private sector provision?

2. What kind of early years services is Jill's group providing for children and their families?

3. How do the church subsidise the cost of the playgroup?

Private sector services

Early years services available from the private sector include nursery schools, playgroups, crèches and childminding services. These organisations provide childcare and early education services to young children who have needs that are not met by the limited range of statutory sector services. Private sector services for children and families are businesses that charge fees to those who use them. A child's parents must:

▶ be able to afford to pay the fees charged

▶ or have the fees paid by their employer

▶ or be eligible for government funding.

Some private sector childcare services are not available to people who might need or benefit from them because they can't afford the costs. However, employers will often **subsidise** childcare for their employees, and government funding is available to all families to obtain pre-school places for children from the age of 3.

Some children's carers also work in their own homes on a self-employed basis. Registered **childminders** are the largest group of self-employed carers working in this way. Like all self-employed carers, they charge the people who use their services a fee for their time and expertise.

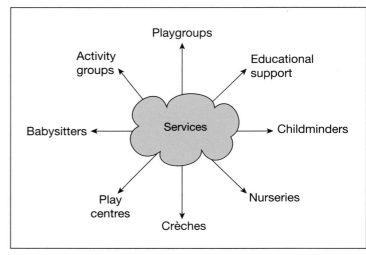

Figure 6.5 Examples of private sector services

Informal early years provision

The majority of childcare and family support is provided by parents and other relatives in the child's own home on a voluntary, unpaid basis. This is known as informal care provision. Caring for children is widely seen as a family responsibility in the UK. Parents who provide informal early years care for their children may also use statutory, voluntary or private services to supplement their own childcare. Additional or specialist input from trained childcare and early learning practitioners may be needed if a child has special needs (learning, health or developmental) or to give a child opportunities to play and socialise with other children.

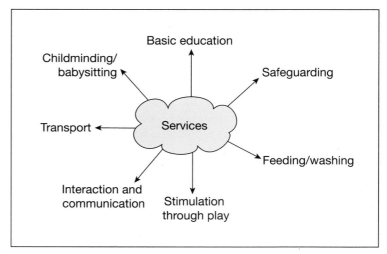

Figure 6.6 Examples of early years services provided informally

Over to you!

Have you ever provided any informal care for a brother or sister, or other young relatives? What kinds of things were you expected to do as an informal carer?

Activity

Imagine that you work for a recruitment agency that provides private childcare services for families with children under 5. You have recently been asked to recruit a nanny to work for a family with two children – a 3-year-old boy and a 1-year-old girl. The family have asked you to produce a list of the skills and personal qualities that an excellent nanny should have. They want to use this in the job description for the post. Your task is to produce this list and then create a short advert that could be used in a local newspaper or in the window of the recruitment agency to attract the right person.

Topic check

1 Which two types of care provider make up the independent sector?
2 Give an example of a large, national voluntary organisation that works with children and families.
3 Describe the kinds of childcare and family support services that may be offered by small, local voluntary groups.
4 Identify three ways in which parents can pay for private childcare services.
5 Who are the providers of informal childcare and family support services?
6 Describe two ways in which independent sector services for children and families are different from those provided by statutory sector organisations.

Children with special needs

Getting started

This topic focuses on the different kinds of special needs children can have and ways of meeting these needs. When you have completed this topic you should:

- know about different kinds of special needs
- understand reasons why some children have special needs
- be able to describe a range of ways of caring for a child with special needs.

Key terms

Cerebral palsy: a group of conditions that are not contagious or progressive, caused by brain damage before or during birth, that result in problems with posture, muscle tone and movement

Congenital: a condition that is present at birth but isn't necessarily hereditary

Disability: a physical or mental impairment that limits one or more major life activities

German measles: a contagious viral disease that can damage foetal development during the first trimester, also known as rubella

Haemophilia: a group of hereditary genetic disorders that impair the body's ability to control blood clotting (and therefore bleeding)

Muscular dystrophy: a group of hereditary, genetic diseases that weaken the muscles and cause problems with movement

Placenta: part of the uterus that provides blood and nutrients for and transfers waste from the developing foetus

Special needs: the additional needs for help and support that a child may have because of health, learning or developmental problems

Spina bifida: a condition in which the foetus's spine does not form properly that can result in loss of sensation and severe muscle weakness in the lower part of the body

Children with special needs

A child with **special needs** has the same basic needs as other children. However, they will also require additional support or assistance to meet their health, learning or development needs. This can be because the child has:

▶ a **disability**

▶ learning difficulties and developmental delay

▶ health or emotional problems.

Congenital disability

Some children are born with a disability. This may be caused by:

▶ an inherited genetic disorder such as Down's syndrome, **haemophilia** or **muscular dystrophy**

▶ a birth accident or trauma, such as oxygen deprivation during labour, leading to **cerebral palsy**

▶ foetal development problems resulting from the use of alcohol, drugs or cigarettes by the child's mother during pregnancy, or from the child's mother contracting a disease such as **German measles** during pregnancy.

Smoking during pregnancy

When women smoke during pregnancy, the ability of the blood to carry oxygen to all parts of the body is reduced. This affects the flow of blood to the **placenta**, which feeds the foetus. Mothers who smoke during pregnancy have a greater risk of suffering a miscarriage. Women who smoke tend to give birth to premature or underweight babies who are more prone to upper respiratory tract infections and breathing problems. The risk of cot death among these babies is also increased.

Foetal alcohol syndrome

A child whose mother drinks alcohol while she is pregnant may develop foetal alcohol syndrome (FAS). FAS is associated with abnormal growth and mental retardation. Mental retardation occurs because the alcohol consumed by the child's mother disrupts the formation and survival of nerve cells in the foetus's brain. FAS is the most common cause of non-inherited mental retardation in the UK. The consequences of foetal alcohol syndrome include:

▶ abnormal facial features

▶ reduced growth

▶ central nervous system abnormalities

▶ impaired learning and memory skills

▶ behaviour problems, such as hyperactivity.

 Case study

Tania, aged 19, is 7 months pregnant. She has been admitted to the Women's Centre at her local hospital because she has developed pre-eclampsia (high blood pressure). This is dangerous because it can lead to convulsions (fits) and reduced blood supply to the placenta. Tania has been feeling a bit dizzy, restless and has a headache. As a result, she has decided to go outside and have a cigarette. The midwives on the ward discourage all of the women admitted there from smoking whilst they are pregnant and do not allow any smoking in the Women's Centre. Tania has smoked an average of ten cigarettes a day throughout her pregnancy and is unwilling to give up.

1. Identify three risks associated with smoking during pregnancy.

2. Describe the effects of smoking on Tania's unborn baby.

3. Explain why Tania is putting her own health at risk by smoking during her pregnancy.

Physical disabilities

A child with physical disabilities may have special needs because they have problems with mobility, coordination or sensory impairment (deafness, visual impairment or speech problems). Examples of physically disabling conditions that result in special needs include the following:

▶ **Spina bifida** (lack of fully formed spine) – can result in paralysis of the lower limbs, bladder and bowel incontinence and learning difficulties.

▶ Cerebral palsy – results from damage to part of the brain controlling muscle function. This condition can result in problems with fine and gross motor control, epilepsy, incontinence, delayed growth and curvature of the spine.

Autism

Children with autism experience communication difficulties. Boys are much more likely to have autism than girls. Children with autism also tend to have learning difficulties, speech and language problems and difficulties with social interaction and relationships.

Down's syndrome

One in every 1000 babies is affected by Down's syndrome. There are approximately 60,000 people living with Down's syndrome in the United Kingdom. The condition is caused by an extra chromosome in the body's cells. It disrupts cell development resulting in the distinctive physical characteristics of people who have Down's syndrome. Down's syndrome affects all ethnic groups and males and females equally. People with Down's syndrome have learning difficulties and may develop health problems, such as heart defects, hearing and sight problems, and an increased risk of contracting infections. A woman who has a child after the age of 35 has an increased risk of giving birth to a child with Down's syndrome.

Attention deficit hyperactivity disorder (ADHD)

ADHD is a disorder in which a child has a short attention span, restlessness and over-activity, short temper, mood swings and very high energy levels followed by fatigue. ADHD is seen by some doctors as a behavioural disorder that is caused by physiological problems. The causes of ADHD are unknown and the diagnosis is controversial. One of the reasons why ADHD is controversial is that doctors frequently prescribe drugs, such as Ritalin, for children given this diagnosis.

Activity

Find out how parents and health professionals can support children with disabilities by watching a video at www.nhs.uk/Conditions/Spina-bifida/Pages/Introduction.aspx.

Activity

Watch the video about Emily at www.nhs.uk/Conditions/Downs-syndrome/Pages/Introduction.aspx. Try to identify the health issues that Emily has faced in her life so far.

Activity

Use the internet, library or other resources to investigate the symptoms and explanations given for ADHD. Summarise your findings in a table that describes the main features and at least two different explanations for ADHD.

Equal opportunities and special needs

Every child is entitled to have good learning opportunities provided for them and should receive the range of services required to meet their needs and promote their development. However, families who have children with special needs often have to struggle and fight to obtain the educational opportunities and support services their children require.

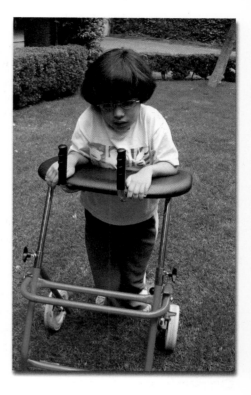

To ensure that children with special needs have equal opportunities, parents, carers and educators have to identify the specific needs of each individual child. Schools and local authorities have legal responsibilities to carry out needs assessments for children who have developmental or health problems. A needs assessment may identify that a child has additional support needs in some areas (e.g. mobility because of spina bifida) but that they are very capable in other areas (e.g. learning).

A child identified as having special needs should have a full needs assessment to ensure that the support for their general development is provided. Focusing purely on providing support for mobility problems might, for example, neglect the child's social and emotional needs, which may be affected by their lack of mobility. Some children with special needs require temporary assistance and support while others require ongoing, more complex input because of more enduring and severe disabilities.

Caring for children with special needs

Families with children who have special needs require, and are entitled to, a range of services.

The birth of a child with special needs can have a big impact on the lifestyle, relationships and support needs of their family. For example, a child with special needs may:

▶ require hospital treatment or other specialist care on a regular basis

▶ need adaptations to be made to the family home or car to meet their particular needs

▶ require specialist equipment that has to be accommodated and used at home

▶ have specific care needs that take up a lot of their parents' time

▶ need more time and attention than their siblings because of their special needs

▶ not be able to go on holiday or day trips because of their special needs, restricting the activities of the family.

However, children with special needs should not be seen as a burden on the family. Families learn to adapt to their child's special needs and often form especially close, supportive relationships with each other as a result.

Support services

A child with special needs may have additional support needs. These are usually assessed by the local authority to identify the individual child's requirements. Statutory services include welfare benefits, housing, education and social services.

Welfare benefits include:

▶ carer's allowance if the child needs constant care

▶ Disability Living Allowance (DLA) for children with mobility problems

▶ help with the cost of transport (to hospital or school, for example).

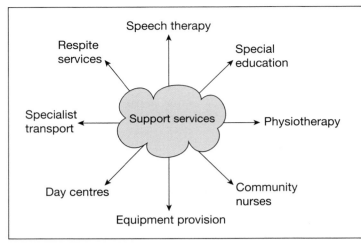

Figure 6.7 Support services for children with special needs

Families with children who have special needs also get priority on housing waiting lists and in primary school application procedures. Local authorities will adapt housing to meet a child's needs and schools have specialist staff and educational support for children with special needs. Local authority children and families departments also provide a range of family and educational support services – particularly guidance and information – to assist families and ensure children have good learning and development opportunities.

Voluntary organisations

A number of local and national voluntary organisations exist. They provide specialist services for children with special needs. These include MENCAP. Voluntary organisations help special needs families by:

▶ giving specialist information

▶ offering practical help and support for families

▶ assessing needs and making referrals to statutory services

▶ providing support groups and day care centres

▶ providing respite care.

Respite care

Respite care is a form of support that allows families to take a short, temporary break from caring for their child. Families who care for children with special needs, particularly those with complex physical disabilities, are likely to use local respite services. Respite care packages usually involve the child being given overnight accommodation and daytime activities by trained carers while their parents or carers take a break from caring for them. Parents and carers need these breaks because caring for children with complex special needs can be very tiring and demanding.

Case study

Malachi is a 7-year-old boy with complex physical and learning disabilities. He developed these problems as a result of being starved of oxygen during his birth. Malachi lives at home with his parents and sister most of the time. He has a specially converted and equipped ground floor bedroom at home. This enables his parents and two carers who come to look after him at times, to provide appropriate care for him. Every 3 months Malachi has a week-long respite break at Sunnydown Hall, a residential centre for children and young people with disabilities. Malachi enjoys

these breaks because he gets lots of attention from the staff and is taken into the hydrotherapy pool everyday – his favourite thing! Malachi's parents sometimes go on holiday or simply stay at home and use the extra time they have to relax.

1. What is the purpose of sending Malachi on regular respite breaks?

2. Who benefits from the respite breaks that Malachi has?

3. Describe two ways in which a respite break might be good for Malachi.

Learning opportunities

Children with special needs require good learning opportunities to maximise their development. They tend to progress at different rates to other children. A child with special needs may benefit from special early intervention programmes that are designed to boost or speed up their development in the pre-school years. A child with special needs may also need speech therapy and physiotherapy, and have home education support. Many children with special needs attend a local school and receive help from classroom assistants. Others attend special schools with facilities adapted to a range of special needs.

Over to you!

Is there a special school for children with special needs in your local area? Try to find out about the range of services and facilities provided at the school.

Activity

What are the advantages and disadvantages of a child with special needs attending a mainstream school? Carry out some research into this issue and produce a table outlining what you see as the advantages and disadvantages of mainstream education for children with special needs.

Topic check

1 Identify three congenital conditions and explain why each may lead to a child having special needs.
2 Why is it inadvisable for a woman to smoke or drink alcohol during pregnancy?
3 Describe the effects of a physical disability on a child's ability to meet their needs independently.
4 What impact can Down's syndrome have on a child's development and abilities?
5 How can the parents of a child with special needs ensure they receive equal opportunities?
6 What is respite care and how is it used to support the families of children with special needs?

7 Controlled assessment guidance

 Getting started

This chapter focuses on the two types of controlled assessment, or coursework, activities that you have to complete as part of your OCR GCSE Home Economics (Child Development) award. When you have completed this chapter you should:

- know about the two forms of controlled assessment you have to complete
- understand what you are required to do as part of your child study task
- know what is required of you in the short tasks.

Key terms

Conclusions: decisions, judgements or opinions

Informal care: care provided by partners, relatives, neighbours or friends

Justify: provide a reasonable and acceptable explanation based on evidence and clear thinking

OCR: the awarding body (examinations board) responsible for providing your GCSE Home Economics (Child Development) award

Reference details: the details of a book (author's name, book title and publisher), TV programme or other source of information

Secondary research: gathering information from existing resources, such as books, DVDs and statistical charts

Completing coursework

You are required to produce four different pieces of coursework for the internally assessed part of your GCSE Home Economics (Child Development) award. **OCR**, the examinations board, sets the coursework tasks and requires you to complete:

▶ one child study task (worth 30 per cent of the overall marks)

▶ three short tasks (each worth 10 per cent of the overall marks).

Altogether, the three pieces of coursework count for 60 per cent of your final mark. You will also need to sit an exam, which counts for the remaining 40 per cent of your final mark.

The child study task

This task requires you to identify and study a child aged 0–5 years of age. It should take you about 22 hours to complete the whole task. There are a number of parts to the task as you will need to use research/investigation, planning, observation and evaluation skills to complete it.

Ideally, you will already have some experience of babies or young children and will be used to spending time with them. This may be the result of having a young sibling, niece or nephew or because you have had a work placement or **informal care** experience with young children. Previous experience will help you with your coursework. It is also advisable to have covered the course content on physical, social, emotional and intellectual development before you begin this assessment task.

Your child study task will include sections on:

▶ research

▶ selecting and planning observations

▶ carrying out and recording observations

▶ outcomes

▶ **conclusions** and evaluation.

With your tutors support and guidance, you will need to work through each of these sections to produce your child study task for assessment.

Research

In this section of the child study task you will need to:

▶ choose one of the OCR set themes to focus on and produce a task title for the research

▶ give clear reasons for your choice of task title

▶ carry out **secondary research** on the chosen area

▶ explore your chosen child's background to obtain relevant information

▶ explain how the task will be carried out.

It is important to identify a child who you can gain information about. You will need to explain to the child's parents what your child study task will involve. They will have to give their full, informed consent before you begin any observations. You will also need to produce a clear title relevant to the development themes that you want to focus on. Your title, and the development theme itself, should be relevant to the child's stage of development. Your tutor will be able to provide you with advice that should help you to choose an appropriate area of development to focus on. However, you will need to be able to explain your reasons for choosing a particular focus and the title of your child study task.

Over to you!

What experience do you have with babies and young children? Make a list of the different occasions, experiences or relationships you have, or have had, that might be helpful in preparing you for the child study task.

Over to you!

Have you thought about any aspects of child development that you might want to focus on as part of your assessment? Your first step will be to identify a child whom you can observe. Can you think of anyone who might let you observe their child?

Activity

Sally, aged 15, has two cousins who are 6 months and 3 years of age. Her aunty says that she would be happy for Sally to observe one of her cousins for her GCSE child study task. Sally would like to focus on physical development. Luke, her 6 month old cousin has started to roll over and reach out for toys. She is a bit concerned that he hasn't developed many other physical skills yet. Lily, her 3-year-old cousin, has good physical abilities and is learning to ride a bicycle. However, Sally's teacher has told her to be careful about choosing an older child like Lily for her observation.

1. What kinds of physical development is Luke likely to experience over the next 6 months?

2. Why should Sally be careful about choosing to observe the physical development of a child as old as Lily?

3. Which child and aspect of physical development would you recommend Sally focuses on?

Secondary research

Background information relevant to your chosen area of development can be obtained from a range of sources (see Figure 7.1).

You will need to be selective about which sources you use and will probably not be able to make use of all of the information you obtain. Your review of the background information that you find should identify the relevant and useful aspects of it. The review should provide information on how a child in your chosen age range ought to have developed and what they should be able to do.

Searching for and reviewing secondary information sources can be time-consuming and absorbing. One of the dangers is that you will get confused about where you found particular items of information. As a result, you will need to be careful about recording your information sources and should obtain the **reference details** for any sources that you do use in your final piece of work. Overall, the background information that you obtain from secondary sources will be used to help you to compare your chosen child's development to the developmental 'norms' or expectations for a child of the same age.

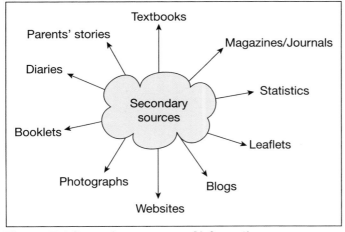

Figure 7.1 Secondary sources of information

Case study

Sally, aged 15, has decided to observe the physical development of her cousin Luke who is 6 months old. She will observe his movement, focusing closely on gross motor skills, holding toys and sitting up, over the next 3 months. Sally now has to carry out secondary research to find out what a child of Luke's age should be able to do between 6 and 9 months of age.

1. Identify three different sources of information that Sally could use to find out about the development of movement skills between six and 9 months of age.

2. Suggest two things Sally could do to keep a record of the information sources she uses.

3. Explain why Sally needs to find and summarise background information on the movement skills of 6–9-month-old babies for her child study task.

Selecting and planning observations

In this section of your child study task you will need to:

▶ recommend possible ideas and activities that would be suitable for the age of the chosen child

▶ select and **justify** ideas and activities to observe

▶ consider suitable methods of carrying out observations

▶ select, and justify the methods you choose for carrying out observations

▶ show a variety of methods to record the results of your observations

▶ produce a clear plan for the observations that you intend to carry out.

Your secondary research should give you a good idea about what your chosen child should be able to do. From this you will need to identify possible areas for observation and make a decision about what your observations will focus on. Figure 7.2 gives an example of possible areas of observation if you choose physical development as an area for observation.

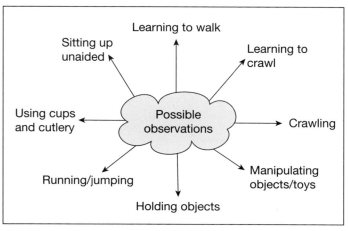

Figure 7.2 Physical development – possible activities to observe

You will need to justify your decision to observe particular features of the child's development. In particular, you will need to explain why these areas of observation are best suited to the particular child you are observing. The final part of your planning should involve developing ways of recording information during your observation sessions. This could involve producing some charts, checklists or forms that you can complete either during or after you have spent time observing the child. You should include examples of your observation records in the planning section of your final piece of work.

Activity

Imagine that you are in Sally's position. You have decided to carry out some observations focusing on Luke's ability to hold toys and sit up. You are going to see Luke for a couple of hours in a few days' time. Your teacher has asked you how you are going to record your observations.

1. Suggest two ways of recording observations about Luke's ability to hold toys and sit up.

2. Produce an observation record sheet that you could use if you were observing Luke.

3. What are the advantages and disadvantages of recording your observations a) as they happen and b) shortly after the observation session?

Carrying out and recording observations

In this section of your child study task you will need to:

▶ carry out the planned observations

▶ demonstrate a range of different methods of observation

▶ record your results clearly and use ICT where appropriate.

You will need to use a variety of observation methods and a number of ways of recording and presenting observations to maximise your grade in this task. Statistical graphs (such as bar charts, pie charts and line graphs), examples of a child's drawing or handwriting, photographs of the child, and your own written accounts and checklists of observations can all be included. Each should show what the child can do.

Activity

You will need to use a variety of observation methods and a number of ways of recording and presenting observations to maximise your grade in this task. Statistical graphs (such as bar charts, pie charts and line graphs), examples of a child's drawing or handwriting, photographs of the child, and your own written accounts and checklists of observations can all be included. Each should show what the child can do.

Outcomes

In this section of your child study task you will need to:

▶ review the observations you have undertaken

▶ show your understanding of the areas of development identified

▶ relate information gained to your earlier secondary research

▶ offer original thoughts and opinions about what you have observed

▶ explain how the child you have observed compares to developmental norms

▶ compare your chosen child's progress with that of other children.

Remember to comment on and explain your findings in detail. This is very important to gain good marks. You will need to show that you understand your chosen child's abilities and can relate them to developmental norms for their age. You should also comment on how the child has progressed during the period you have been observing them. Again, linking this to developmental norms is the best way to show your understanding. Most marks are gained from showing clearly that you understand what you have observed.

Conclusions and evaluation

In this section of the task you need to do the following:

▶ Review all aspects of your work, identifying strengths and weaknesses in each area of the child study.

▶ Identify and justify any changes you made to your plans while carrying out the child study task.

▶ Draw conclusions referring back to your task title. You should give your own view about what you have learned from carrying out the task.

▶ Make recommendations for improving your work and for further work that could be carried out to develop your child study.

▶ Demonstrate good spelling, punctuation and grammar in your written work. You should also try to use the specialist language and terminology of child development wherever possible as this will improve the clarity and preciseness of your writing.

Your conclusion should demonstrate understanding of your chosen area of development and show that you can apply this to your chosen child. You need to be clear and honest about both the strengths and weaknesses of your work. You need to comment on how successful you have been and must draw logical conclusions from your evidence. Remember to list all of your sources in a bibliography – including a list of websites – at the end of your report.

Good luck with your child study task!

The short tasks

You will need to complete three short tasks as part of your GCSE Home Economics (Child Development) award. These short tasks are chosen from a list of OCR-set task titles. You will need to choose one task from the investigative task list and two tasks from the practical task list.

You will be assessed on your ability to:

▶ plan each task

▶ carry out practical work

▶ present and explain outcomes

▶ evaluate your work.

Planning the task

You will need to show your ability to:

▶ make and justify suitable choices in response to your chosen short task title

▶ produce accurate plans and identify suitable resources for implementing your choices for carrying out the task

▶ plan and produce (or select if appropriate to the task) methods for recording your results (e.g. questionnaires, testing, comparison charts, costings).

Practical work

You will need to show your ability to:

▶ follow your own plans, making good use of the time available

▶ organise your resources effectively

▶ use equipment safely and independently

▶ demonstrate a range of skills, which might include ICT skills (producing a leaflet, use of graphic data), costing and comparison/testing

▶ include written evidence to support the work carried out.

Outcomes

You will need to show your ability to:

▶ produce one appropriate, well presented outcome linked to the area of study

▶ accurately carry out and record the results of your findings.

Evaluation

You will need to show your ability to:

▶ identify the strengths and weaknesses of all aspects of the short task

▶ suggest and/or justify improvements in your work

▶ draw conclusions from your work.

Index